"I've seen the prophetic accuracy of Jeremiah Johnson in my own life. There is a new breed of prophets coming that are going to take us as the Body of Christ to a new realm of authority. Read this book and pick up that spirit."

-Lou Engle
Author and Founder of The Call

"Based on my interactions with both Loren and Jeremiah, I'm more than happy to commend them to you as solid ministers who love Jesus and His Bride. In *The Micaiah Company*, they share a healthy combination of heartfelt observations and prophetic insight—a sobering reality check for the prophetic movement that will hopefully facilitate a much-needed course correction. If something you read here makes you mad, search the Scriptures and ask the Lord if it's true. Regardless, you'll have a hard time finding two authors who share a deeper passion for genuine, high-quality prophetic ministry in the Church. And for this reason, it is my joy to recommend this book."

-Art Thomas
Missionary-Evangelist, Filmmaker, and Author

"I feel honored to be asked by my friend, Loren Sandford, to write an endorsement for the new book that he is co-authoring with Jeremiah Johnson, called "The Micaiah Company: A Prophetic Reformation". As I read through the manuscript, it became clear once again that Loren speaks as a father in the prophetic movement.

As a father he has watched its rebirth and is now observing it as it grows and develops. What I sense from what Loren shares is the valid concern at this stage in the prophetic movement, that it could get snuffed out before it has a chance to begin to mature. I trust Loren's voice and insight on the prophetic because he speaks not as a critic from the outside, but as a concerned member of the broader pro-phetic family and flows in prophetic ministry himself.

One of the obvious concerns of both Loren and Jeremiah is that the prophetic movement has not just been called to tickle the hearts and souls of people in the church, but that it is also called to speak into the world. Loren also knows and respects the written word of God which has served as his standard to weight everything by. As you read this much needed new book, you also will come to appreciate their hearts as well as their mature and loving voices speaking wholeness into this ministry from the Lord."

-Fred Wright
Founding Coordinator for Partners in Harvest, An International Family of Churches birthed out of the Revival in Toronto, Canada
    Author of the highly acclaimed book, "The Four Great Revivals" as well as "The Power of Thanksgiving", both published by Catch the Fire Publications.

The Micaiah Company
A Prophetic Reformation

Jeremiah Johnson and R. Loren Sandford

Scripture quotations are from the New American Standard Bible, copyright 1995 by the Lockman Foundation. Used by permission.

ISBN: 1536864315
ISBN 13: 9781536864311

Cover Design by John Burton
Cover Art by Ruslan Solntsev (c) 123RF.com

To order copies of this book in bulk quantities, or find out where Jeremiah Johnson and R. Loren Sandford are ministering next, please visit our website at www.themicaiahcompany.com

Dedication

To the Micaiah Company…

May you find strength, encouragement, and comfort in the following pages. You were born for such a time as this.

Contents

Foreword

JEREMIAH JOHNSON AND my son Loren Sandford, in their book *The Micaiah Company*, have called for desperately needed changes in the prophetic movement – and beneath that, persistent death of self in seeking intimacy with our loving Lord Jesus Christ (only that which can birth and sustain such needful changes) – and repentance and revival in the church across the world. I could not agree more fully.

Paula and I were forerunners in the rebirth of the prophetic movement, mainly through teaching and down-on-the-knees prayer, and through our books, *The Elijah Task* and its sequel *Elijah Among Us*. Many thousands have responded and prophets have become widely known throughout the body of Christ, and to some extent, the world.

But though we taught about more than ten basic functions of prophets, unfortunately the one function of giving personal prophetic words has become so popular that many think that's all there is to being a prophet. More disappointing and grievous to us is that, as Jeremiah and Loren so poignantly document here, such personal words have all too often become mere unsanctified psychic readings that pander to the people's carnal desires – to be successful, famous, powerful, etc. People crowd and jostle one another to get into places in audiences where they hope to receive a word "from God". Paula and I have grieved about this almost to the point of wishing that we had never pioneered the movement! Paula has gone home to her reward, but I am grateful beyond measure for this book by Jeremiah and my son Loren.

Jeremiah and Loren rightly castigate the current error that says that prophetic words must always be positive and encouraging – people somehow also deluded into thinking that rebuke and correction are not themselves positive and encouraging! Reproof from God is pure love for us, but that seems to be too little understood.

Years ago, while still in the pastorate, I was walking to the church, praising God that He is always so loving and kind. Instantly, I heard Him speak, strongly and even sarcastically, "You love your picture of me!" I knew He was telling me I would not let myself see the stern side of Him. From then on, He began to reveal Himself in all the many biblical passages about His judgments, His angers, and His disciplining of those He loves. That understanding, and its biblical passages, went into *The Elijah Task,* but has largely fallen into oblivion as this generation's Pollyannaish view of God has grown so dominant. I pray that this book by Jeremiah and Loren will gain such popularity that the reality of God's sternly loving nature can be seen again.

Jeremiah and Loren lament that prophetic pronouncements of God's will to discipline His own are so often not spoken, and if said, receive so much rejection. Some time ago, I said to God, "Father, You urged Paula and me to teach that a good and wise father appropriately and firmly disciplines his children in love. You are the best Father there ever was. Now, the body of Christ is sinning wildly, and we do not see You disciplining Your children! Why?" His answer broke my heart! God said, "My children have walked so far away from Me that I cannot treat them as sons and daughters and discipline them as I want to" (Hebrews 12:5-8). One of the greatest tragedies of today is that God cannot treat us as sons and daughters and discipline us for our good! Therefore, we wander apart into greater and greater troubles and sins.

Can we see here the truth of Loren's assertion that only if there is deep enough repentance and consequent revival in our churches can there be a return to true prophecy – or to Christ-like behavior for that matter?

One final comment: Jeremiah and Loren speak of the judgments of God, and our unwillingness to hear about judgments prophetically. God's judgment is to brood over His creation as His Spirit did in the beginning. Whatever is amiss, His first judgment is to act to correct and heal, lovingly. But when our unrepentant hearts do not allow Him to act redemptively, then He must act ever more sternly and, to us, painfully in personal judgments. His personal stepping in to bring painful happenings is intended to awaken us to the truth of where we are, and cause true repentance. When we will not heed His personal actions to recall us, His judgment then becomes impersonal, the reaping of the whirlwind of destruction that that we have sown, without the grace of His interventions to spare us (Hosea 8:7). This is not His will but due to our stubborn resistances and failures to repent, our loving Lord then has to abandon us to reap what we have sown. Due to our stubborn resistances and failures to repent, we then have to learn the hard way what His grace would have written on our hearts the easy way.

Jeremiah and Loren warn that we are failing to heed God by rejecting corrective prophecies. We are preventing His corrective words, drawing nigh to that time when despite what our loving Lord wants, we will have to reap destructions. They pray for the Micaiah Company to arise, and plead for us to hear. The impersonal devastating reaping of what we have sown is drawing nearer every day.

I pray, fervently, that the message of *The Micaiah Company* will be heard before it's too late.

Lest I be seen as a prophet of doom, let me assure that my hope has not yet died. My hope is that enough – ten righteous in any city? – will respond, and our country – and the world – will be turned back to God. And that true prophets will play the part God intends – the call of God to speak His words, and the call upon us to repent, as this fine book trumpets so clearly.

John Loren Sandford
Founder, Elijah House International

Introduction
(R. Loren Sandford)

I (LOREN) SELDOM receive revelation by means of dreams. It's just not my "way". Many years ago, Bob Jones spoke a word over me that went, "I have my little dreams and visions, but you're a Nathan prophet. You just know things." This has been mostly true for me over the years. I have often said that if you have the Father's heart, then you know what He knows. Obviously, that statement is not an absolute, but it makes a valid point. I've therefore made it my life's quest to absorb the Father's heart and make it my own. If I speak accurately, it flows from that source. If I don't, then I missed His heart. It's that simple.

When, therefore, I have a dream that has a "God" sense about it, I pay attention. November 15, 2015 I had the following dream. John Paul Jackson (founder of Streams Ministries and a spiritual son to my father) came to me (no I don't speak to dead people – it was a dream) and I found myself in a kind of counseling session with him, as if he were seeking my help, pouring out his grief over what he saw going on in the prophetic movement. Things needed to be fixed and changes needed to be made in order to correct mistakes. His grief flowed first from the mistakes that have been made, and then from the sense that he could no longer address the issues and bring healing.

In every part of this vivid and colorful dream I felt reality. I knew in the dream that John Paul had passed away, so it felt like his spirit had come to me to pour out the kind of grief you would feel when you can't go back to fix anything that you know caused hurt or damage. The dream included a part 2, the specifics of which I couldn't remember when I woke up, but I know that it had something to do with action I needed to take. A mantle of responsibility had been passed to me.

Some years ago, I had a discussion with a friend of mine about problems in the prophetic movement. At that time, he served as the international coordinator for a major movement of churches in revival. Because of his position of leadership and his connection with hundreds of churches internationally, he was and remains in a uniquely strong position to observe trends in the body of Christ. As we talked, he stated flatly, "If something isn't done soon, the prophetic movement is dead in five years."

More than five years have passed since that meeting in my living room. He was wrong in his prediction of the death of the movement, but not in his concerns. A crisis has developed in the prophetic movement and it grows by the day. It may be that the emperor is nearly naked, but few people have yet noticed or had the courage to point it out. Jeremiah and I – Jeremiah a young 20-something, and I an old guy in his mid-60s – have collaborated on this book, two generations together, because our hearts ache for what we see. For the sake of the Lord, we cherish the gift and the office of prophet and we want to see it operate in purity to benefit and strengthen the body of Christ.

I have no doubt that we will make some enemies because of this book. Offense will be taken as we threaten or question commonly held assumptions and ministry practices. I'm certain that some will accuse us of arrogance. I will be surprised if we escape being criticized for being critical, although our hearts are certainly not in that place. We plead only that the reader seek out the truth in what we say, and, if you disagree with some – or much – of what we have written, then God bless you. We love you anyway.

1
The Problem We Face
(Jeremiah Johnson)

WE LIVE IN critical days for the prophetic movement. I believe that without a decisive and significant course correction, we are headed for imminent destruction/shipwreck. In many circles in which I currently travel, prophetic ministry has become not only a laughing matter among church leaders, but is considered unreliable and inaccurate by a growing number of disillusioned saints. We are witnessing one prophetic word after another fall to the ground from well-known prophetic voices and no one is held accountable or even offers to repent for their mistakes. In other circles, prophetic ministry has become so politically correct that any prophetic words of warning, rebuke, and correction are categorically rejected. Where have we gone so wrong in the prophetic movement? At what juncture did we run off the tracks and fail to ask, "Where is the prophetic movement headed?" Or do those in the prophetic movement even care about their current reputation in the body of Christ? Are we content with the way things are and are we ultimately blinded to how far short we fall from biblical and accountable prophetic ministry?

God's Answer
I believe that God's answer to the crisis currently facing the prophetic movement is the "Micaiah Company". These are prophetic voices that

will not go with the status quo. Many of them, right now, are engaged in a battle for their destiny. In 1 Kings 22 Micaiah initially echoed what the other prophets of his day were saying, but when pressed by the hand of God, he knew that he had to deliver the word of the Lord, regardless of whom it offended and what kind of platform he would lose.

I believe there are many Micaiahs all over the earth, still undecided as to where their allegiance lies. Will they echo along with their contemporaries what the people want to hear, or will they walk in the fear of the Lord and deliver to the people what they need to hear? Make no mistake, the path of the Micaiah Company is a road less traveled, full of rejection and loneliness at times, yet it's a path of glory filled with the affirmation and applause of the Father. It's time for the Micaiahs in the earth to come out of hiding and get off the fence. These are the days when you will finally recognize why you were created. You indeed were born for such a time as this!

The Days of Jeremiah

We must come to terms with the current state of the prophetic movement in order to discover and discuss real solutions to the issues before us. Much of what we are witnessing in the contemporary prophetic movement mirrors the days of Jeremiah. Prophets are prophesying falsely, leaders are leading with their soulish authority, and the people of God LOVE IT SO (Jeremiah 5:31)! Yes, I quoted that verse correctly. Like Micaiah, Jeremiah lived in a period of time when the contemporary prophetic movement of his day had created a culture in which people actually loved false prophecy! They loved to hear words that tickled their ears, but had no depth or substance. So called "prophets" claimed to speak the word of the Lord, yet God had not sent them. When inquiring of Jeremiah as to what the burden of the Lord was, Jeremiah told the people, "YOU are the burden," says the Lord.

The Deception

The contemporary prophetic movement in America has fallen in love with soulish prophecy and promoted church leaders who cater to their selfish ambitions and desires. We tend to cry out for more pro-phetic voices who will confirm to us our carnal wishes and dreams and then lead us to sow big money into their ministries, telling us that we will be blessed financially for doing so. We buy their books and sit at their feet. Our incredible lack of discernment has built their platforms and granted them permission to continue on in deception and flattery.

The truth is that in many of these meetings and arenas, a com-pany of Micaiahs is hanging out in the background. They watch the success of these contemporary prophets and then observe the response of the people. An incredible inner struggle goes on inside of them. They cry out in the night, "God, I just want to fit in! Why can't I just mimic and parrot what's going on out there right now?" As these words leave their lips, the fear of the Lord overtakes them. This Micaiah Company knows deep down inside that they cannot compro-mise the word of the Lord. In their heart of hearts, they long to find other Micaiahs just like them. They search for others who can easily move a crowd with their prophetic gift, but yet refuse to prostitute the anointing on their lives.

Calling the Micaiah Company

I want to sound the alarm in the prophetic movement. It's time for the Micaiah Company to arise! Many of you have picked up this book because you know that there must be more and I'm here to declare to you that there is indeed more and there are others just like you who are sick and tired of what people are calling "prophetic ministry". You know that there is a strong prophetic call on your life, but you just can't seem to find any contemporary prophetic voices that you agree with. You are wondering if you should just give up because your life would be so much easier. I say to you, *Rise up, the Lord is with you, mighty warrior.*

If you are eager to discover what the "Micaiah Company" is all about, I believe that the rumble in your spirit will be articulated in the coming pages and it will cause a fire to be kindled inside of you like never before. Behold, a prophetic reformation is coming to the earth and it starts with you and with each one of us. We must in humility confess the faults and errors of the contemporary prophetic movement and ask God for His grace and forgiveness to make things right. The "Micaiah Company" is being birthed and assembled in the earth right now. Are you one of them?

2
Micaiah Versus The 400
(R. Loren Sandford)

IN MY TRAVELS and online I encounter increasing numbers of people disillusioned with the prophetic movement at a time, unfortunately, when a critical need exists for solid prophetic ministry, not just for the sake of individual lives and destinies, but for the redemption of nations and cultures. Too many prophecies have gone unfulfilled, dates have been set and missed, catastrophic events have been predicted that never happened, promises have been made that didn't unfold, and there have been moral failings on the part of well-known prophetic leaders, as well as a growing number of biblical imbalances and violations. All of this takes an increasing toll on confidence in the prophetic gift and it has led some to begin to think that the prophetic gift is not for today. Too much of the prophetic movement has gotten it wrong or wandered off base. Credibility and confidence have been eroded.

Jeremiah has already referred to I Kings 22 when Jehoshaphat and Ahab convened 400 prophets to seek the will of the Lord concerning engaging in battle to retake Ramoth-Gilead from Aram. Four hundred prophets read the desire in the hearts of the kings, listened to a deceiving spirit (22:22-23) and told them what they wanted to hear, "Go up to Ramoth-Gilead and prosper, for the Lord will give it into the hand of the king."

Micaiah alone heard the voice of the Lord and knew the truth, but initially succumbed to pressure to speak in unison with the 400. Only when Jehoshaphat commanded him to do so did he relent and speak what he really knew from the Lord. "I saw all Israel scattered on the mountains, like sheep which have no shepherd. And the Lord said, 'These have no master. Let each of them return to his house in peace'" (22:17). He continued, "Therefore, hear the word of the Lord. I saw the Lord sitting on His throne, and all the host of heaven standing by Him on His right and on His left. The Lord said, 'Who will entice Ahab to go up and fall at Ramoth-Gilead?' And one said this while another said that'" (22:19-20).

Apparently, a prophetic movement was underway in Israel such that 400 so-called prophets could hold a convocation. Who in that day who truly heard God's voice would have had the courage or the confidence to disagree with the dominant stream, especially with a word that didn't sound particularly positive or encouraging? Micaiah stood alone against two kings and 400 acclaimed prophetic voices only to suffer humiliation when Zedekiah slapped his face for not joining with the majority (22:24). He then found himself imprisoned and fed sparingly on bread and water (22:27).

In the world of the prophetic, Micaiahs don't often stand out in the crowd. Their words tend to get lost in the blizzard of prophecies coming from the 400 who speak what the kings want to hear. In fact, established prophetic ministries regarded as gatekeepers in the prophetic world will often reject them outright and shut them out. In I Kings 22:24, Zedekiah the son of Chenaanah not only slapped Micaiah's face, but mocked him as well, ""How did the Spirit of the Lord pass from me to speak to you?"

Micaiahs don't run with the herd. As a result, the herd doesn't like them very much. And yet, a growing number of pastoral leaders and everyday members of the flock hunger for plumb line prophets like the Micaiah Company to speak a grounded, solid word from the heart of God that passes the test of Scripture and reveals the nature of Jesus.

As Jehoshaphat did, you may have to seek out the Micaiahs. You may even have to cajole them into speaking what they know - again as Jehoshaphat did - because they know that if they speak the truth of what they have heard from the Lord, the response won't be pretty. While Micaiah sat in prison being fed on bread and water, paying the price for his faithfulness, the kings ignored his counsel, lost the battle and King Ahab died.

Ultimately, four hundred "prophets" had it wrong. The prophetic movement of the day failed catastrophically to serve the need of the hour. Apparently, prophetic agreement among a group of recognized prophets is no guarantee that the prophetic word actually comes from God. The kings chose to act on the voice of the majority, Israel suffered defeat and Ahab was killed.

Today an incident like this might cause many to reject prophetic ministry altogether. In fact, I know of pastors, leaders and lay people who once believed in contemporary prophetic gifting who have already rejected it as valid for today. Of even more concern is the fact that the majority of the body of Christ would fail to heed the lesson and would never learn to recognize the accurate voice. They would therefore continue to listen to the 400, in spite of their record of failure, and they would continue to ignore the Micaiahs who speak the not-so-popular truth. Fortunately, regardless of consequences to Ahab and the army when 400 prophetic voices missed it, Israel didn't scuttle prophecy as a ministry. Rather, because one outnumbered prophet had it right, prophecy continued to be regarded as a valid ministry both in Israel and, later, in the church.

It would seem that the key lies not in how many are speaking a particular word, but in discernment to know who is actually speaking from God's heart. Do we have a dearth of real discernment in the church today? Are we too ready to hear only what excites us and what we want to hear? Have we accepted the unbalanced – and therefore false – teaching that the only valid prophetic words are positive and encouraging ones? More on that later! Have we relegated true prophetic voices - who are ever the minority - to the sidelines and locked them up because they refuse to speak with the voice of the majority or because their words aren't what we like to hear?

History is replete with occasions and seasons when the truth has rested not with the dominant word spoken by the majority, but with the less popular minority. These voices seldom enjoy wide respect or acclaim. They threw Jeremiah down a well and disregarded his words. Elijah was called the troubler of Israel whom Jezebel, the king's wife, sought to kill. And so it went!

Maybe we need to stop listening so intently to the popular voices who speak with the mainstream. Could it be that a purified remnant speaks a plumb line word that doesn't win them the platform of wide-spread popularity? Can we discern the word of God in a hidden, but emerging generation of prophetic voices who might not speak what we want to hear, but who certainly speak what we need to hear? In doing so, might we be more edified and better prepared for the glory to shine out in a fresh outpouring of the Holy Spirit in the midst of a gathering darkness? Might we also be not only encouraged, but confronted with our sin and impurity? Would that not position us more effectively in love and power for the difficult and eternally strategic days that certainly lie ahead?

The problem of the 400

As opposed to Micaiah's ability to accurately hear the word of the Lord, what mistakes did the 400 make? What influences led them to draw the wrong conclusion? The answers to these questions cut to the heart of the crisis we face today in the current prophetic movement. I'll add others, as well, that might not be an integral part of the incident reported in II Kings 22, but that certainly affect us in the current season.

I can honestly say that more than 90% of prophetic words spoken over my life and ministry have not come to pass. At this writing this stretches over forty years of professional ministry. Inaccurate in detail, in substance and in the unfolding of actual events, they flowed from the hearts of men and women truly dedicated to God, many of them on the prophetic A-list, but who clearly weren't hearing God's voice. Across my nation and the world, untold thousands of good people who deeply love the Lord bear the same kind of testimony. For some, this has led to bitterness and disillusionment, and, in some cases, abandonment not only of the idea of prophetic ministry, but even of the church itself. Others have done the right thing in the face of prophetic failure and have directed their hearts to God with more purity of focus than before.

A lifetime of living with prophetic ministry, first in growing up with a father who pioneered the prophetic movement, then in laboring under the burden of my own calling, has led me to a set of simple conclusions reflected in the Micaiah situation and in other passages of Scripture.

A Faulty Prophetic Model

You purchase a car. It turns out to be a lemon. You're angry and frustrated, but you don't therefore reject the idea of "car" and decide never to drive one again. Rather, you figure out what is wrong with that particular model and then go shopping for one that reflects the quality you have a right to expect. Similarly, when prophetic ministry goes wrong and you receive a bad word or see that popular predictions of national or world events have not come to pass, you can be hurt, angry or disillusioned. You don't want to conclude, however, that prophetic ministry itself is wrong and then shut your heart to that kind of input. Rather, wisdom would recognize that perhaps the model itself was faulty. This would lead you to begin to search the Word and the heart of God for the shape of the real thing and you would look for the prophetic voices that best represent that truth. Prophetic ministry itself is not the problem, but often the model in which it comes.

Over-emphasis on personal prophecy from a public platform

We have been conditioned by a self-centered and self-absorbed culture to hunger after personal blessing. As a result, we have twisted nearly every ministry of the church to serve that focus. Observing current practice, you would think that the primary thrust of prophetic ministry is for the gifted one on the platform to call people out of the audience to give personal words. In fact, in many places this has become the very definition of what we regard as prophetic.

Unfortunately, this often creates an atmosphere akin to white witchcraft. People gather, not to hear the life-changing prophetic word addressed to the whole people of God that would separate the precious from the vile and establish a unified direction focused on Jesus and His kingdom, but to be personally served, encouraged and even flattered. I will never forget a meeting of pastors and leaders I attended in 1988 at which John Paul Jackson was slated to minister. As worship came to a close, two or three hundred people waited for him to take the stage, each one longing for some word to be directed at them personally. To John Paul's everlasting credit, he refused to take the stage that day. He rather sent word that the spirit of the audience was all wrong. If memory serves, he used the phrase "white witchcraft". The meeting ended there.

While we have made personal prophecy from the public platform the dominant model, it hangs from the slenderest of threads scripturally. The only clear word of personal prophecy publicly given in the New Testament came when Agabus warned Paul that if he went to Jerusalem he would be arrested and bound (Acts 21:11). I am convinced that he did this openly in front of the whole church, rather than privately, because Paul's leadership role as an apostle affected the whole church. It was a way of preparing the whole people of God for a difficult time of loss.

I Corinthians 14:30 has often been construed as support for the current dominant model. "But if a revelation is made to another who is seated, the first one must keep silent." I would suggest that this had much more to do with simply revealing truth and insights to one another about Jesus at a time prior to the establishment of the New Testament than it does with the sort of thing we do today.

Personal prophecy is legal. Don't get me wrong! Witness Nathan confronting David with his adultery with Bethsheba and the murder of her husband, Uriah. Notice also that this was done in a private setting and in the implied context of a relationship between the two men. I myself seldom give personal words from the public platform unless it involves the lives and ministries of leaders who then affect the whole flock.

Sanctified psychic reading

I'm convinced that the 400 truly believed they had received the word of the Lord. In truth, Jehoshaphat and Ahab drew from the 400 what they wanted to hear. Four hundred prophets sensed what was in the hearts of the kings, failed to discern the difference between the true word from God and what they sensed in the desire of the kings, and then spoke it out as prophetic direction. That failure cost Ahab his life in the ensuing battle.

This kind of misfire occurs in nearly every prophetic circle I have experienced as people believe that the prophet has revealed some secret or fact specific to them that only God could know. Not so. The so-called prophet has only demonstrated that he or she is a prodigy at reading the hearts of people. The resulting prophecies often reflect, not words from God, but rather desires and goals in the heart of the recipient or even the desire of the prophet to impress or garner praise for a "good" word. Obviously, stellar exceptions to this dynamic exist, but too often the same failure that led Ahab to his death creates serious problems in the lives of people today.

Ability to read the hearts of others does not make one prophetic. It merely makes one fully human with a fully alive human spirit breathed in by Father God at conception. In the natural, barring disability, all of us can walk. Some of us can run, while others of us are prodigies at running to such a degree that we win races. In the same way, each of us with a fully functioning spirit, alive and awake, can sense the hearts of others. We do it all the time. For instance, we enter a room and pick up on the mood of the place before a word is ever spoken. Most of us can easily sense when a person is hiding something or is untrustworthy. Similarly, we often meet people we instinctively trust long before that trust has been proven. Subtle elements of body language contribute to this, but it's much more than that.

As with those who are prodigies at running, some of us are prodigies at this kind of sensing. We mistake this for prophetic gifting when it's really just a form of psychic reading. Lives then suffer destruction when the so-called prophet on the platform reads the ambition, the longing or the hurt in someone's heart and then reflects it back as a word from God, failing to differentiate between the heart of the individual and the word from heaven. The prophet fails to recognize the difference between the sources of what he or she is sensing and then believes that what he or she senses in the individual is itself the word of the Lord.

This kind of reading the hearts of people can be a wonderful ministry tool for compassion and for connecting with people, but until coupled with a true prophetic function, it is not prophetic. Sense the person, then ask the Father to speak in relation to it. Simple formula! Add to this the erroneous and unbiblical idea that all New Testament prophecy must be positive and encouraging and you get the kind of deception that actually does damage rather than good in the long run.

You get the untalented, ungifted songwriter, for instance, with a horrible voice who is told by the "prophet" on the platform that he will stand in front of thousands with his music. You get the man who derails his successful career to sell his home, move to another state and invest everything he has in attending a ministry training school, only to find himself in frustration and despair because he has neither the gifts nor the calling for the pastoral ministry the so-called prophet told him he would have. People too often receive words concerning great destiny that are more reflective of their own needs and ambitions than the true will of God.

Stealing God's words from one another

"'Therefore behold, I am against the prophets,' declares the Lord, 'who steal My words from each other'" (Jeremiah 23:30). The first element of this is that human emotions form a lens that magnifies and distorts the word of God as it passes through. Many inaccurate and off balance words delivered by so-called prophetic people start with a truth but end as a falsehood because of failure to sort out personal feelings, desires and emotions from the true word of God. Where does God end and "me" begin?

The true word comes from the heart of God, a heart never in turmoil. The center of God's heart will always be a place of peace, rest and love - fruits of the Spirit - even in His wrath or grief. God *is* love. No word should ever be spoken that does not flow from that place of rest and love, even when the word contains warning and judgment. Never mistake adrenaline flow for the anointing of God or confirmation of a word. I have often said that excitement is the mother of bad judgment. This is especially true in prophetic ministry.

When the prophet allows excitement, anger, ambition or any other emotion to infect or drive the prophetic word, error results. False dreams and visions spring from this polluted fountainhead, like the ones in Jeremiah's day among those who did not want to see their nation destroyed in the flames of judgment. Human fear caused them to reject the true word of the prophet and led them to dream instead of deliverance and victory. "'Behold, I am against those who have prophesied false dreams,' declares the Lord, 'and related them and led My people astray by their falsehoods and reckless boasting; yet I did not send them or command them, nor do they furnish this people the slightest benefit,' declares the Lord" (Jeremiah 23:32).

Under this dynamic, one prophet might speak a word that generates some form of excitement. The next one picks it up and, in his excitement, builds upon it. Thus the word grows with each sharing until it no longer resembles anything the Lord has truly spoken. This can happen with positive words and it can happen when negative words of judgment generate another kind of emotion.

To coin a term, I think we need to practice "zero-based prophecy". I don't want to know what other prophetic voices are saying about an issue until I have sought the Lord for myself and heard from Him. I want to avoid building on the words of someone else because those words caused me to be excited. Once I have heard for myself, I might compare what I have heard with what others are getting, but I'll be seeking balance and understanding, not to build upon what I've been given.

I suspect that when a conference of 400 prophets came together to speak to Ahab and Jehoshaphat about taking back the land they felt belonged to them, there came a sense of excitement they interpreted as the Spirit of God. Often the purely human dynamic of the energy generated by a large crowd is mistaken for the anointing. The 400 therefore read the hearts of the kings, allowed emotion to carry them forward, mistook it for anointing and thus made themselves vulnerable to a deceiving spirit that felt like the voice of God (I Kings 22:22).

It is past time for us to cease being carried along by current trends, words and teachings. It is past time for us to stop confusing that rush of adrenaline or the excitement of the moment with the true word from God. It is long past time for us to root ourselves deeply in intimacy with our Lord and in the foundation of the written and eternal Word of God.

Failure in grounding

Too many who pose as prophetic people in the body of Christ today operate from an inadequate base in the eternal written Word of God, relying instead on supernatural experiences and feelings. Paul warned in Colossians 2:18 against taking a, "stand on visions he has seen, inflated without cause by his fleshly mind." Charismatics, those who believe in the gifts of the Spirit, have often been justly accused of biblical ignorance and poor theology. We too often fail to balance and test experience against the solid foundation of the unchanging Word of God.

As a result of all this, unbiblical doctrines and practices have infected many segments of the body of Christ and have shaped the words of those who pose as prophetic voices. This is not the place to attack most of these issues. I point it out merely to illuminate a source of prophetic inaccuracy and delusion. I wrote at length concerning tests of the true prophetic word in *Understanding Prophetic People*. Every accurate prophetic voice recorded in the Bible understood the Scriptures as they were available to them at the time. This gave them a filter through which to pass perceptions and to test the accuracy of what they believed they were hearing.

As a result, Jeremiah knew the Lord at a level of fullness that his contemporary Hananiah did not (Jeremiah 28). Isaiah expressed the heart of God in both promise and judgment in ways that many others of his day completely missed. The apostle Paul prophesied accurately, representing the true heart of God and the meaning of the Jesus events with profound insight and accuracy because he knew the Scriptures better than anyone of his generation.

It's time for us to get it right. Prophetic ministry is not a game. Lives and eternal destinies hang in the balance.

3
Deceptive Misconceptions – Part 1
(R. Loren Sandford)

IN *UNDERSTANDING PROPHETIC People* I wrote at length about what prophetic ministry is not. Here, however, I'm focusing on just a few key contemporary misconceptions concerning what constitutes prophetic ministry that I believe have contributed greatly to the current crisis of imbalance.

Mystical experiences do not equate to prophetic gifting
In nearly six decades of living in the prophetic soup – my parents were baptized in the Spirit in 1958 when I was seven years old - I have consistently seen people fascinated and wowed by prophetic words couched in supernatural or mystical terms. In fact, if it doesn't come from a dream or vision of some kind, the word may very well be ignored. This has resulted in a skewed focus and has deafened too many Christians to the voices of prophetic stability. We tend to equate prophetic gifting with mystical awareness and supernatural experience. Scripture makes no such equation. Yes, some prophetic revelation comes through such experiences, but more often than not, it comes in much less fascinating forms.

When we focus on mystical experiences and being supernatural, we aggravate the problem created when human emotion forms a lens that distorts the prophetic word as it passes through. Too many prophetic voices seek to exercise the gift from an experiential base with insufficient biblical grounding. Words are then inadequately tested biblically, and the result is inaccurate prophetic words, false teachings and heresies. Equally problematic is the dearth of teaching concerning wilderness crushing and shaping of character, without which the prophet cannot adequately test the word by the character of God or represent the nature of the One from whom the true word flows.

The current widespread quest for, and emphasis on, supernatural experience in renewal and revival circles feeds this imbalance. I have often written and stated openly that if your focus is the supernatural you will end up in shipwreck, but if your focus is on intimacy with Jesus, you will end up walking in the supernatural.

Yet, even that formulation cannot work without the discipline of character forged in the fire of wilderness testing, together with such a depth of scriptural grounding that the very spirit of the Word of God has been deeply implanted. "For the word of God is living and active and sharper than any two-edged sword, and piercing as far as the division of soul and spirit, of both joints and marrow, and able to judge the thoughts and intentions of the heart" (Hebrews 4:12).

Dreams. Visions. Angelic visitations. Translations to heaven. Feelings and senses. All valuable! But on close examination, such experiences actually appear to be a relatively small portion of the biblical record where prophetic inspiration is concerned. In fact, you will find these mystical elements mostly concentrated in apocalyptic passages in portions of Daniel, parts of Ezekiel, parts of Zechariah and the book of Revelation. Among the prophets of the Old Testament, Ezekiel would rank as one of the most mystical for his visions and mystical encounters with the realm of the spirit, but regardless of the frequency and intensity of such experiences when compared to Isaiah or Jeremiah, Ezekiel is not considered a greater prophet than Jeremiah or Isaiah. Similarly, at no point does the biblical record indicate that the apostle John (author of Revelation) - whose Book of Revelation was almost entirely a set of mystical visions - should be considered more prophetic than the apostle Paul who rarely spoke from vision or dream.

Scripture rather shows prophetic people diligently seeking the mind and heart of God, but not necessarily with a specific experience in mind. Nothing in the text of Revelation, for instance, indicates that the apostle John actively sought to be caught up in dramatic visions. Scripture says only that he was "in the Spirit on the Lord's day" (Revelation 1:10) and that God sovereignly chose to visit him with powerful heavenly visions. He didn't climb up to the Lord on his own initiative. Rather, the voice of the Lord invited him up, "Come up here" (Revelation 4:1).

Unfortunately, in the church today we see a strong trend toward seeking ways and means to generate these experiences by our own enterprise. We tend to exalt those who have these experiences, and who then tell us about them, as if they were more holy, more spiritual, more gifted or more prophetically reliable than others. This is a dangerous imbalance and an improper focus. Better to hunger after simple and pure intimacy with the Holy Spirit than to focus on any given result of that intimacy or on some method for receiving revelation! In Scripture, prayer, fasting, meditation and worship seem to be the key means of finding the intimacy I speak of.

The prophet Isaiah told of his great Temple vision in Isaiah 6, but in the remainder of the book by his name, such visions are neither a dominant feature of his prophetic revelation, nor are they presented as his primary means of receiving words from God. The call to Jeremiah in Jeremiah 1:10 included no promises of mystical experiences. God simply declared in Jeremiah 1:9, "Behold, I have put My words in your mouth." I would suggest strongly that He did this through the Holy Spirit by means of character adjustments and upon the foundation of Jeremiah's careful study and deep understanding of the scriptures available to him at the time. In a lifetime of study, dedication to the Lord and attention to the Law of Moses, as well as the historical books of God's dealings with His people, Jeremiah took into himself the substance and sense of all that God had revealed of Himself up until that time. This prepared him to hear the voice of the Lord in an intimate, practical and natural way.

Two causes of imbalance

Prophets spin out of balance for two reasons. First, our natural sense of intuition predisposes us to be open to supernatural experiences of all kinds. By itself this not only poses no real problem, but can actually be a boon to our ministry. In no way am I opposed to supernatural experiences. I only caution against making the quest for supernatural experiences a focus.

The problem arises with the second reason. When we become caught up in, and fascinated by, supernatural experiences, it becomes too easy to anesthetize the pain so many of us prophetic people bear as we sense and carry the suffering in the world around us. This can lead us to subconsciously long for the experiences themselves, like taking a drug, rather than for genuine and simple intimacy with God. I suggest that this constitutes a form of idolatry.

By seeking mystical or supernatural experiences in an unbalanced way, whether that be vision, dream or trance state, we render ourselves vulnerable to delusion and demonic counterfeit. Unless the initiative rests with God alone, we enter into the realm of the occult.

God will indeed grant us supernatural experiences, and I love it when He does, but isn't it much better to aspire after intimacy with the One who gives us those experiences as He chooses to give them? "For in many dreams and in many words there is emptiness. Rather, fear God" (Ecclesiastes 5:7). Having a mystical or supernatural experience, no matter how powerful, is not the same as intimacy with God. We must not, therefore, actively seek after visions or employ any method or approach to produce them by our own initiative. Shouldn't we rather long to be included in the intimate counsel of the Lord who sometimes sovereignly chooses a vision, dream or supernatural encounter as one means of conveying His counsel? Let God alone choose the means by which He speaks at any given time.

In Acts 8:40, did Philip seek to be teleported over a considerable distance in a moment to appear where God wanted him to be? Doesn't this rather appear to be a sovereign act of God as opposed to something Philip went looking for by any prayer or method of his own? Philip had been with the Ethiopian eunuch on the road to Gaza. God urgently needed him at Azotus, and therefore acted sovereignly to move him there by His own means and for His own purposes.

Adjust the focus

For many years now I have heard and seen prophetic people writing and speaking openly of their "third heaven" experiences. Caution is in order! The apostle Paul wrote II Corinthians 12:2-4:

> I know a man in Christ who fourteen years ago whether in the body I do not know, or out of the body I do not know, God knows such a man was caught up to the third heaven. And I know how such a man whether in the body or apart from the body I do not know, God knows, was caught up into Paradise and heard inexpressible words, which a man is not permitted to speak.

We ought to seriously question how many of these "third heaven" experiences are biblically legal to present for public consumption. Too often this creates an unhealthy fascination with supernatural experiences not normal for the average believer, or even for many prophetic people. This diverts attention from more important, more essential elements of the Christian walk, such as greater revelation from the light shed by the mystery of the cross, the power of God's infinite love and the need for a pure and humble heart in intimacy with God.

I say again that I do love mystical experiences. I am in no way rejecting that kind of encounter with God or that vehicle of revelation. At the end of one 24-hour prayer session a number of years ago, I found myself literally paralyzed by the power of God, helpless on the floor for an hour and a half, my face and extremities completely numb while His power penetrated and healed me. I could only lie there and weep. Three times angels have visited me. On two occasions they came to deliver words from heaven concerning guidance, instruction and deliverance. Once, an angel visited me for healing after a surgery. Although I love experiences like these, I have determined never to seek any such encounter by any initiative of my own or by any learned method originating with me. The initiative for such experiences lies with my God and flows from His wisdom concerning the best way to communicate with me at any given time.

In truth, many who claim to have such experiences on a regular basis are neither prophetic nor holy but have simply exposed themselves spiritually by some human approach or by means of natural abilities to sense things in the realm of the spirit (note the small "s"). Never has the mere experience of a supernatural encounter been an indication of holiness or intimacy with God. Spiritual experiences are common to witches, warlocks, New Agers, shamans and witch doctors. These people understand and practice various kinds of methods to thin the veil between the physical and spiritual realms by forms of human effort, but the spirits they hear from are neither angels nor God.

In Samaria, Philip encountered Simon who "formerly was practicing magic in the city and astonishing the people of Samaria, claiming to be someone great; and they all, from smallest to greatest, were giving attention to him, saying, 'This man is what is called the Great Power of God.' And they were giving him attention because he had for a long time astonished them with his magic arts" (Acts 8:9–11). Clearly, Simon knew how to produce psychic and supernatural experiences, and did it for money, but when Peter intervened in Acts 8:21 to respond to Simon's request for the gift of the Spirit, he said, "You have no part or portion in this matter, for your heart is not right before God."

God can and does use mystical experiences to communicate revelation and often does so with prophetic people. Never, however, should we equate ability to experience mystical things in the spirit with prophetic calling or ability, although many genuinely prophetic people do experience such things, some of them frequently. I merely plead for us to leave the initiative with God and for us to hunger rather for essential intimacy with Him with or without transcendent mystical encounters! I plead for character formation rooted in the cross in union with Jesus and for a pure hunger to be intimate with Him. Into such a framework, He can pour any experience He sovereignly chooses without bringing about imbalance and dangerous delusion.

More on "Sanctified Psychic Reading"

Every one of us has a personal spirit breathed into us by our Creator God. Of the many functions of our personal spirit, one of the most essential is the ability to be able to sense others. Call it compassion, if you will. The word means "to feel with". Through the personal spirit breathed into us by God, we've been given, as a birthright, the ability to feel with one another through a divinely created interconnection.

In light of this, speaking of the Holy Spirit (different than our personal spirit) Paul said, "For by one Spirit we were all baptized into one Body, whether Jews or Greeks, whether slaves or free, and we were all made to drink of one Spirit" (1 Corinthians 12:13). The Holy Spirit is the baptizer and the body of Christ is the medium into which He immerses us. Then in verse 26 he spoke of the awareness we enjoy through this connection, "And if one member suffers, all the members suffer with it; if one member is honored, all the members rejoice with it." In our personal spirit we can sense others. When the Holy Spirit indwells us in union with our personal spirit, an even larger sense of connection results. In Galatians 6:2 he commanded us to "bear one another's burdens, and thereby fulfill the law of Christ." Not only can we do this in the Lord, but we do it naturally every day. It's how we're made!

As the Holy Spirit quickens us, however, we become more alive in our personal spirit, more alert and more sensitive to the hearts of those around us. As persons created in God's image, this is our birthright. Life's wounds, sins and the influence of the culture around us can dull or cripple our natural ability in this regard, but it remains the birthright of every created human being. This is a natural ability common to our race that for some us is stronger and more developed. For instance, I'm a musician. I "hear" music. All of us can appreciate music, but some of us, like me, hear it differently and more accurately with all of its nuances, while still others enjoy what we call "perfect pitch". Ability to sense the inner hearts and thoughts of others is precisely like that. Some do it better and with a more acute sense of it.

As already stated, we often exalt people with a heightened ability to do this to the status of "prophet" because we mistakenly believe that they could only know what they know from the hearts, lives and inner thoughts of others if God had told them. Truthfully, any one of us with an alive and active human spirit can sense these things. Any one of us can develop and sharpen that sense as we come alive in our spirit. For instance, while someone might be able to generally sense fear in the heart of a friend, my own senses have been sharpened to differentiate between various forms and causes of fear – fear that came from sexual abuse, fear stemming from physical trauma, fear of loss due to abandonment, and so on. Some of this comes from natural gifting while much of it comes through training my senses through experience over time. Virtually all prophetic people are prodigies at this kind of sensitivity, but not all who move in this kind of sensitivity are actually prophetic.

Trouble comes when we sense ambition, desire or hope in the heart of another, fail to discern whether what we sense comes from a clean place or not, assume that it must be something God is saying, and then present it as a "prophecy" when all we are actually doing is mirroring their own heart back to them. This was at least in part what the 400 did with Jehoshaphat and Ahab, and it ended badly.

Prophecy is words from God to men and women, not a reading of the hearts and minds of men and women by men and women. The true prophetic word flows from intimacy with God on the part of the prophetic person, rather than from personal psychic awareness of the hearts of others.

Our human ability to feel and identify with others at the level of spirit is the foundation of real compassion. This can be a powerful tool for ministry, but must not be confused with genuine prophetic ministry. Great and uplifting prophetic words, on the other hand, can be delivered more effectively when we compassionately identify with the hearts of those to whom we prophesy. When we accurately read what is in people from the human side, and then seek God for the true word in relation to it, powerful things can result.

Discerning the difference between current desires and ambitions we sense in the heart of the one to whom we minister, and the true word originating in the heart of God forms the key to accurate one-on-one prophetic ministry. Maturity, experience, brokenness and humility built into us over time enable us to do this effectively. Unfortunately, too little teaching is available to help prophetic people discern the difference, much less become aware of the need to seek this level of discernment.

In 1 Kings 22, out of 401 recognized prophets, Micaiah alone possessed the depth of intimacy with the Lord necessary to discern the difference between the desire of the kings, his own desire to speak favorably, and the true heart of God. Ahab died because of prophetic failure and his own unwillingness to hear the words of a genuine prophet. Worse, these combined failures opened both the prophets and the kings to the influence of a deceiving spirit (see 1 Kings 22:22). How much that passes as prophetic today stems from the influence of deceiving spirits because the body of Christ doesn't want to allow for or hear the whole truth?

Personal desire and the need to please the kings set both prophet and people up to hear from the enemy of our souls and suffer shipwreck of both life and faith. What I call "sanctified psychic reading" can be a wonderful tool in compassionate ministry under the discipline of the Holy Spirit, but we must never confuse it with being truly prophetic.

4
Deceptive Misconceptions – Part 2
(Jeremiah Johson)

I SEE A growing trend in the contemporary prophetic culture of America in which everything must be positive, politically correct, and performance based or it can't be from God. It is a trend toward releasing and embracing only general encouragement and words full of false hope that often have too little substance or depth. These words sound good in the moment, but carry little weight long term. This shift and crisis in the current contemporary prophetic movement mirrors the shift and crisis that Jeremiah experienced in Bible times. He cried out in agony and prophesied to his peers saying, "you are addressing the wounds of the people superficially. You are crying out, 'peace, peace' when there is no peace'" (Jeremiah 6:14). As in the days of Jeremiah, so too the current contemporary prophetic culture in America largely rejects or ignores calls to repentance, cries for reform, and confrontations of specific sin in the land. Jeremiah went even further to address how the general public would respond to prophetic words that are positive, politically correct, and performance based in chapter 5 at verse 31, "The prophets prophesy falsely, and the priests rule on their own authority; AND MY PEOPLE LOVE IT SO! But what will you do at the end of it?"

Nevertheless, God has mercifully raised up voices in every generation that have confronted trending prophetic patterns. These voices are themselves prophets, but have been called by God to resist and expose the false and immature prophets in the land.

He raised up Leonard Ravenhill in his generation to cry out with great clarity regarding prophetic ministry. He said, "The prophet comes to set up that which is upset. His work is to call into line those who are out of line! He is unpopular because he opposes the popular in morality and spirituality. In a day of faceless politicians and voiceless preachers, there is not a more urgent national need than our cry to God for a prophet!" ("Picture of the Prophet" by Leonard Ravenhill Copyright 1994 http://www.ravenhill.org)

Make no mistake! At this point in history there is a tremendous crisis in the prophetic movement. I dare say that the number of prophetic voices who are actually carrying the legitimate word of the Lord are far fewer than many of us would hope for. In a day and age where the words and heart of the Lord are so necessary and needed in the land, I'm deeply concerned that the contemporary prophetic movement may be headed for strong judgment from the hand of the Lord.

Spontaneous Prophecy

Two types of prophecy exist: *spontaneous prophecy and revelatory prophecy*. All believers are capable of prophesying on a spontaneous level, particularly in small group settings and even in worship. Paul addresses this gift in 1 Corinthians 14:1-5. The saints can bring edification, exhortation and comfort to the body of Christ on many levels. Spontaneous prophecy rarely offends people (it shouldn't) and it finds its roots in encouragement and blessing. Spontaneous prophecy can be given by individuals who are not prophets of the Lord, but who are simply exercising the momentary gift of prophecy. On the other hand, revelatory prophecy can be given only by prophets themselves. While prophets can operate in both spontaneous and revelatory prophecy, ordinary believers who operate in the gift of prophecy are limited to spontaneous prophecy.

Contemporary prophetic culture wholeheartedly embraces spontaneous prophecy. They love and enjoy the general blessing and encouragement that comes through believers who move in the gift of prophecy as well as through prophets themselves. The crisis comes when the only form of acceptable prophecy in the land is spontaneous prophecy. What about revelatory prophecy? Could it be that in labeling believers who operate in spontaneous prophecy as "prophets" that we are actually misleading and bringing confusion to a subject that really needs clarity and direction?

Revelatory Prophecy
Spontaneous prophecy is a valid and intricate part of church life, but revelatory prophecy goes much deeper. Revelatory prophecy is born in the place of prayer and fasting. It then requires days, weeks, and even months of careful prayer and meditation before it is released. Revelatory prophecy by nature is simply too directive, too corrective, and too predictive to be delivered on a whim. If you asked a prophetic voice in America when is the last time that they went on an extended fast before releasing the "word of the Lord" what would they say? If you asked them when is the last time you didn't just receive a "word" and then immediately shotgun it out on Periscope, Facebook, or Twitter, what would they say? Would it be too extreme to say that there is more spontaneous prophecy being released to the body of Christ than revelatory prophecy?

Revelatory prophecy often calls for repentance and warns of the consequences if the word of the Lord is ignored. Words of warning are the Lord's last real attempt to keep us on track or restore us to the right path. Prophets cannot give revelatory words with the same freedom as they do spontaneous words.

The Great Divorce
Is it possible to embrace both spontaneous prophecy and revelatory prophecy? Can we accept spontaneous prophecy that brings general encouragement and blessing as well as revelatory prophecy that calls

for repentance, warns of impending judgment, and shakes regions and nations?

I absolutely think we can and desperately need to!

The foundation for all prophetic ministry is built upon the character and nature of God. Many prophets and prophetic people have no problem acknowledging the God in the Old Testament that executed wrath and judgment when neccessary, but numerous ones have an issue with recognizing the God in the New Testament that disciplines, judges, and corrects, much less that He remains full of wrath and judgment.

I wrote in detail in my book, *I See A New Prophetic Generation*, that Jesus Christ came to be the full expression of every aspect of the character and nature of the God of the Old Testament, as revealed to Moses in Exodus 34. God does not present Himself as a jealous God in the Old Testament who then says, "I will not be that way in the New Testament." Nor did He say, "I am full of truth," in the New Testament and then show Himself not to be like that in the Old Testament. I want to be very clear and transparent: the current pursuit by many prophets in the earth right now to divorce the God of the Old Testament from the God of the New Testament is doing significant damage to the body of Christ.

I believe God is positioning the bride of Christ in this hour to receive His correction, discipline, rebuke and therefore His justice without interpreting it as rejection. His judgment upon our lives is a demonstration of His goodness toward us as His people. The issue is not whether or not He loves us, but whether or not our own orphan hearts can receive His love for us. At times the words of the Father bring great comfort to our hearts and in other seasons His words sting in order to bring adjustment. We must always remember that whether the words comfort or sting, they still come from the same voice of our loving Father.

Let me be clear! While I do not believe that correction and discipline (judgment) are the primary ways God deals with us as His children under the New Covenant, to throw out these aspects of His character and nature altogether and say that the cross of Jesus Christ did away with them is not founded upon the full counsel of God. As prophetic people, we must take careful consideration and observation of ALL SCRIPTURE before we make blanket statements. God is a good and gracious Father, but in His truth and just nature He will bring about correction and discipline for our good. As Hebrews 12:6 says, "For those whom the Lord loves He disciplines and He scourges every son whom He receives."

Distorted and Twisted Views
One of the greatest obstacles and hindrances to prophets and prophetic people accepting a New Covenant God who can and will discipline believers is a distorted view of the cross of Jesus Christ. To say that under the New Covenant there is no more room for judgment - and particularly no more room for the discipline of God upon the life of a believer - is not only biblically inaccurate, but it also brings forth a potentially greater underlying issue - namely that we can become so enamored and obsessed with certain aspects of God's character and nature, that we totally disregard those with the potential to offend.

In some prophetic circles, there is such an emphasis and focus placed on the goodness and kindness of God, that anything in any prophetic word that even remotely speaks of God the Father's ability to bring correction and rebuke as His discipline to His people's lives is almost categorically rejected. Warnings, cautions, and anything whatsoever considered negative is thrown out the window as not being part of New Covenant prophecy. Prophetic words that address specific sins, as well as calls for repentance on a personal, city, or national level are frowned upon because they are considered judgmental. Many believe God is not into that anymore.

When God's warnings aren't positive enough
Several years ago I was ministering to a group of leaders and students who had gone through supernatural and prophetic training from a very popular Christian movement.

While I was preaching, I had a strange spiritual experience where I was shown an assignment from the devil against a particular leader and his wife. I outlined 3 specific attacks that their marriage would face over the next 7 years and assured them of victory as God gave them clear direction of hope in the midst of trial through the prophetic word. I have never felt the love of God for a particular couple like I did that night.

After the meeting, the couple in leadership that I had prophesied over came up to me and said that they renounced everything I said to them because it wasn't positive enough. They said their prophetic and supernatural training had instructed them to not receive any negative words.

Sadly, this couple was divorced within that same year. Isn't it amazing that I was personally encountering the love of God for that couple as I prophesied to them because He was so kind to warn and expose them to the devil's plans ahead of time, yet they failed to receive it because it wasn't "positive" enough?

And trust me, that situation I encountered years ago has been repeated over and over again. Much of the current contemporary prophetic movement is teaching saints to not receive God's warnings and referring to them as "curses", from "the devil", "Old Testament like", and so on.

Can you imagine Noah telling God that the message about the flood wasn't positive enough? Can you imagine Joseph telling God that the dream about the slaughter of infants wasn't positive enough? Can you imagine Agabus telling God that the coming famine wasn't positive enough? How about the 5 out of 7 churches in the book of Revelation who were rebuked and corrected by Jesus Christ Himself?

My prayer for the prophetic movement is that we will simply receive what God has to say, no matter how severe or gentle it is. Why do we continue to create immature prophetic saints who are continually blindsided by the enemy? People are "binding" God's warnings and calling them curses or too negative because they don't really know Him. I have learned how to rejoice when God warns me through His prophets. When the words of warning, correction, and rebuke come, I rejoice! I thank God for His love and kindness for my life. He cares enough that if I'm heading down the wrong path, He will fire warning shots time and time again.

As prophets and prophetic people, if we believe that God as Father is incapable of disciplining His kids, every prophetic word we release, regardless of how a person responds to the truth of God in their lives, will assure them that only blessing and hope are around the corner. Nowhere in scripture does God promise peace, prosperity, and blessing to individuals, ministries, and nations who walk according to the counsel of the wicked.

In other prophetic circles, such an emphasis is placed on the judgment and correction of God, that any word that remotely speaks of God's desire as Father to bring healing and restoration to His people is categorically rejected. Prophetic words filled with destiny, hope, and the promise of revival are thrown out the window because God is now fed up with the sin of the people. As prophetic voices, if we believe that God the Father is incapable of demonstrating His kindness and goodness to His people, every prophetic word that we release, regardless of how a person responds to the truth of God in their lives, will carry an unnecessary corrective and judgmental tone.

The Micaiah Company

The Micaiah Company rising in the earth will not only know God the Father as a good and kind God, but also as God and Father who disciplines because He loves. Whether it's a word of rebuke and correction or a word of affirmation and applause, they will not reject certain aspects of God's character and nature while accepting others. They will not be limited by their personal experience and will take into consideration the full counsel of God as they sit before Him.

As prophetic people, we must ask ourselves, "What aspects of God's character and nature do I currently understand, and therefore am capable of releasing to His people, and what aspects of His character and nature quite frankly make me uncomfortable, and therefore limit me in my ability to minister to His people? Have I had hurtful experiences in the past that prevent me from receiving all of who God is? The Micaiah Company is not only capable of prophesying incredible words of hope, destiny, and healing, but they are also trained in releasing words of correction, rebuke, and calls for repentance.

While prophets and people alike simply cannot fully comprehend this God of the Old Testament and God of the New Testament, the Micaiah Company will carry a rare grace to see them as one. They will testify that Jesus is not only full of grace, but also full of truth. They will testify that God the Father not only loves His children, but loves them enough to discipline them when they go astray. The Micaiah Company will know what the people of God need and when they need it. Just as an earthly father knows what his children need and when they need it, so these prophetic messengers will be keenly aware of the Father's heart and have access to His mind and His emotions.

I foresee indescribable beauty and testimonies too numerous to count as the Micaiah Company travel the earth rebuking and correcting one, while releasing the Father's goodness and kindness to another. You won't have to worry, because to them, they are still representing the same loving Father regardless of how He chooses to manifest Himself. And oh my! How refreshing these messengers will be.

Maturing in the Prophetic

I want to try to articulate as clearly as I can that to continue majoring on certain aspects of God's character and nature and to minor on, or plainly ignore, others is both unhealthy and leaves the prophetic movement greatly limited and ineffective in its impact on the body of Christ. Some prophetic people have an exceedingly great revelation of the kindness and graciousness of God, while others possess an immeasurable grace to deliver words full of correction and rebuke.

We must be very careful not to emphasize and magnify certain aspects of who God is to the degree that the people of God become totally unfamiliar and uncomfortable with other aspects. Whether

God's goodness and kindness make us uneasy or His ability to correct and bring adjustment makes us cringe, we must give ourselves to
allowing God the Father to work into us the aspects of His character
and nature that we do not yet possess. A fully mature prophet will
carry and embrace every aspect of the character and nature of God
and be graced with the ability to deliver at any moment to any individual the portion of who God is that the person is in need of.

We must see prophetic ministry as God inviting His people
through His servants into a full-on participation and encounter with
His character and nature, rather than being spectators of the words
He releases. I see prophetic schools in the days ahead spending way
more time teaching prophetic people about the character and nature
of God, and much less time on the mechanics of prophecy. Our desires
in the prophetic movement to get words of knowledge for people
and various details of their lives to produce a "wow factor" have too
often derailed God's desire to impart His character and nature to His
people. How are people's lives really transformed into the character
of Christ when they leave prophetic meetings talking more about the
prophet than the God of the prophet?

Once again, one of the primary roles of a prophetic voice is to
assist people in their ultimate calling in life, which is to be conformed
into the image of Jesus Christ, the Son (Romans 8:29). In essence, we
have too many prophetic voices ready to tell people what God wants
to do for them and not enough messengers ready to tell people who
God wants to be for them.

I remind you as the reader, that Moses, the leader of Israel in
Exodus 33 and 34, could not have been more ripe for a word of direction and future promises. Most prophetic voices would have jumped
at an opportunity to prophesy to a man leading a million man army,
knowing what God had already spoken! But what did God Himself
choose to release to Moses? His character and nature! It wasn't what
God could do for Moses that would get him to his destiny, but who
God could be for Moses that would grant him access to His destiny.
And let's not forget, God shared all of who He was with Moses. He

did not hide or ignore certain aspects of His character and nature, but rather showed all of Himself to him and even more to us as believers in the Person of Jesus Christ as revealed in the New Testament.

Delivering Corrective Words of Prophecy

While I believe that delivering words of discipline from the Father is reserved for New Testament prophets and not for those who oper- ate in an occasional gift of prophecy, I also believe that corrective words of prophecy should never be delivered spontaneously in a public gathering. I have rarely seen a corrective word of prophecy that was delivered in this manner bear fruit, not only because it was released in the wrong setting, but because it was so vague that it cre- ated more confusion than clarity.

As a believer who operates in the gift of prophecy, if all you ever receive and deliver are words of correction and rebuke for people, you need to go back and read 1 Corinthians 14 and, while you're at it, cry out for a revelation of the character and nature of God. And if you are called to be a New Testament prophet and all you ever release are hard and judgmental words toward leaders and the body of Christ, you must pursue and embrace every aspect of God's character and nature so that those who sit under your ministry might receive a mature and complete revelation of who God is!

Church leadership should not have to worry about some bizarre prophet walking into the back of the church building (and of course no one has ever seen them before) to issue a rebuke to the leader- ship for hidden sin or a number of different issues. This is completely out of alignment with the heart of the Father for the New Testament church. A prophet's behavior should put a ministry team at ease, rather than on the edge of their seats with unnecessary fear. The Micaiah Company have been sent to local assemblies to be blessings rather than create collateral damage!

With all of this being said, I absolutely believe that there is a place for corrective prophecy regarding the discipline of the Lord under the New Covenant, but it must never be given spontaneously and must be delivered only by broken and tested prophets. The issue at stake here for the Micaiah Company is how to effectively steward corrective words from the Father in a way that will bring forth the greatest amount of fruit. Standing up in the back of a church building unannounced and starting to shout or grabbing a microphone and screaming will not have a far-reaching impact upon the saints. Ultimately, it will be destructive rather than edifying to an assembly of believers, which again is not the heart of the Father for the New Testament Church.

Protocol and strategy must be established in a local assembly by church leadership to provide a place for tested and broken prophets to submit corrective words of prophecy. I believe that how we deliver a word must be seen as a key ingredient in the delivery and effect of it. The Micaiah Company are broken vessels that the Father can entrust with strong corrective words for individuals, ministries, and nations, because this is an aspect of His character and nature that He chooses to share with His people. This, as Hebrews 12:10 says, "...is for our good that we may share in His holiness".

I believe with all my heart that an aspect of God's character and nature as revealed in the New Testament is His ability to train, adjust, correct and rebuke, but we must be very careful as the Micaiah Company that we are spending significant time with Him in prayer and fasting to allow Him to work His heart inside of us before we deliver His words. It is not enough to deliver His words. We must deliver them with His heart!

The abuse and misuse of this particular aspect of God's character and nature has done tremendous amounts of damage to the body of Christ and the prophetic movement itself. On the other hand, we are also witnessing an overemphasis on God's goodness and kindness at the expense of emphasizing His ability to discipline and bring correction to His body. This happens, in part, because so many prophets that have gone before us have prophesied out of their flesh and not from spending time standing in the counsel of the Lord to allow His character and nature to be fully formed inside of them.

I believe that in order for the prophetic movement to put childish ways behind them and truly grow up in this hour, we are going to have to stop allowing the extremes of our past experiences to dictate our present and future beliefs concerning who God is and how we are to minister His character and nature to His people. Just because the prophets of the past may have prophesied about a God who was angry when really He was full of delight, does not mean we should currently prophesy about a God who is pleased when really He is upset or vice versa. As the Micaiah Company, we must set aside extremes and even our own experiences and go on a journey to discover His character and nature as revealed in His Scripture. It is only through spending time with Him that we will carry an accurate revelation and interpretation of who He is and release it to the saints.

We desperately need clarity and revelation in the contemporary prophetic movement if we are going to navigate through the current crisis. We must begin to embrace and receive the Micaiah Company who move in revelatory prophecy and carry words that will shake cities, regions and nations. As previously stated, I believe the way in which we choose to release this revelatory prophecy, especially in the local assembly will have a large impact on the fulfillment of it.

Bring on the spontaneous and general encouragement! I love it! We need more of it! But, oh how we need the word of the Lord that corrects, instructs, chastises, warns, rebukes and releases the fear of the Lord. Let's embrace the gift of prophecy that any believer can move in that seeks to edify, exhort, and bring consolation, but let's also embrace the ministry of the prophet found in Jeremiah 1:10 that roots out, pulls down, destroys, and overthrows. This is the counterbalance and reformation that the contemporary prophetic movement so desperately needs. If we will position ourselves in the American Church to receive both spontaneous and revelatory prophecy and seek to welcome the Micaiah Company in our midst, I believe there is hope for the contemporary prophetic movement.

5

A Plea For Balance

(R. Loren Sandford)

AS JEREMIAH HAS noted, currently gaining ground in spiritual renewal circles is the idea that all prophetic words given today must be positive, encouraging and uplifting. Anything not fitting into that box tends to be rejected. But where did we get the idea that prophetic words in New Testament ministry must always be positive, uplifting and encouraging? Is that really the biblical ideal and standard? If it is not, then what essential benefits are we being cheated out of? As in the days of Micaiah, how many genuine prophetic voices are being sidelined and silenced?

Part of the answer to why this imbalance has become so popular lies in the emotional filters and attitudes through which we pass our understanding of contemporary prophecy and even of Scripture itself. These can create dangerous imbalances in what we believe to be allowable or proper in prophetic ministry. When we read Scripture passages selectively and out of context, we build theologies, rules and boundaries around what our emotional state or inner condition prepares us to hear and allow, and we cherry-pick what we like while ignoring the rest.

Several theological fallacies undergird this current inadequate definition and limitation of what prophetic ministry is and does. These weaken the power and impact of what passes as prophetic in the current prophetic climate. The first and most important is a misunderstanding of the role and ongoing authority of the Old Testament. The second is an unbiblical extreme view of grace that fails to represent the fullness of who Jesus is. The third is a misunderstanding of the meaning of judgment in both testaments and the heart of God behind it. Jesus as Judge is just as much the God of love as is Jesus the Savior.

These theological fallacies inevitably lead to failure to present the fullness of the nature of Jesus – such a tragedy given the fact that the spirit of prophecy is the testimony of Jesus (Revelation 19:10). Above all, the prophetic voice should reveal the fullness of the nature of the Godhead. If prophetic ministry is to have anything like the effect God intends, then we must present and reflect the fullness of who the Father, Son and Holy Spirit truly are.

Still another theological fallacy stems from a failure to examine the full sweep of New Testament prophetic ministry and the tendency to pull certain passages, such as I Corinthians 14, out of their defining context. We'll take each of these in turn.

Old and New Testaments

Let me state it plainly. Jesus absolutely did not set aside or negate the Old Testament. Long have major segments of the church failed to understand the truth of what it means that we are now under grace rather than law. In light of this, too many have been taught to believe that the Old Testament no longer applies. A false contrast has been created that says the Old Testament is law and the New Testament is grace. Law versus grace, however, has to do only with the means by which we receive salvation, not with the truth or eternal validity of the revealed Word of God. God does not change. His will, His morality and His principles embedded in Scripture therefore do not change and cannot therefore be set aside or abrogated.

This being true, we must recognize that what the Old Testament teaches regarding prophetic ministry applies to New Testament ministry as well. In fact, some things taught in the Old Testament are not repeated in the New Testament, not because they no longer apply, but simply because they were already written and regarded as authoritative by the New Testament authors.

Where prophetic ministry is concerned, only one difference between Old Testament and New Testament applies. The governmental authority of the Old Testament prophets such as Samuel - who represented the kingship of God on earth and exercised governmental authority - becomes the authority of the apostle in the New Testament. In that sense, prophetic authority under the New Covenant takes a step down. While Old Testament prophets stood over nations and kings in authority, New Testament prophets stand *under* appointed church authority set over them. Study the references to Agabus in the Book of Acts and you will see that he never gave a command. He rather informed leadership so that leadership could decide what to do.

Regarding the authority of what we call the Old Testament, Jesus said:

> Do not think that I came to abolish the Law or the Prophets; I did not come to abolish but to fulfill. For truly I say to you, until heaven and earth pass away, not the smallest letter or stroke shall pass from the Law until all is accomplished. Whoever then annuls one of the least of these commandments, and teaches others to do the same, shall be called least in the kingdom of heaven; but whoever keeps and teaches them, he shall be called great in the kingdom of heaven. (Matthew 5:17-19)

Because we couldn't perform it, Jesus abolished the Law as the means to salvation. His sacrifice on the cross set us free from the curse of our failure and made grace through faith the way. He did not, however, negate the Old Testament as the expressed heart and will of the Father. Further, it wasn't the Law itself that so upset Jesus. He objected that the Pharisees had failed to discern the heart of the Father expressed in it. They had therefore made of it something far from the intent with which God gave it. At root, the Law was a legal system designed to govern an agrarian society thousands of years ago. That culture no longer exists. Jesus revealed and taught the principles and the true intent embedded in the Law that would apply to any generation or culture in order to reveal and enforce the Father's loving heart.

It was always love and it was always grace! One need only read the stories of the failures of men like Abraham and David, to name just two, in order to see that the Old Testament was not law as over against New Testament grace. God does not change. It was always grace. This is why Paul wrote:

> Therefore do not be ashamed of the testimony of our Lord or of me His prisoner, but join with me in suffering for the gospel according to the power of God, who has saved us and called us with a holy calling, not according to our works, but according to His own purpose and grace which was granted us in Christ Jesus from all eternity, but now has been revealed by the appearing of our Savior Christ Jesus, who abolished death and brought life and immortality to light through the gospel" (II Timothy 1:8-10).

And from the apostle John we get this: "For the Law was given through Moses; grace and truth were *realized* through Jesus Christ" (John 1:17). Grace was neither inaugurated nor instituted with the death and resurrection of Jesus. It was rather "revealed" and "realized". It existed in the heart of God and in his dealings from eternity. Grace expresses who He was, is and ever shall be. Law versus grace cannot legitimately be used to negate the Old Testament.

The apostle Paul, the great grace teacher, also wrote: "All Scripture is inspired by God and profitable for teaching, for reproof, for correction, for training in righteousness; so that the man of God may be adequate, equipped for every good work" (II Timothy 3:16-17). He could only have been referencing the Old Testament since the New Testament had yet to be written, and he clearly affirmed the value of the Old Testament scriptures for equipping men and women of God for life and ministry.

All of this is to say that we can and must learn from the Old Testament. We must not limit what we know of the nature and practice of prophetic ministry to a scant few New Testament verses, often taken out of context. Apart from the whole counsel of God contained in both testaments, we cannot possibly understand the fullness of the prophetic task.

Prophets and the problem of judgment

In the current climate, given our failure to regard the Old Testament with the same reverence as did the apostles, it would seem somehow illegal for anyone to deliver a word that might sound like judgment. Everything must be edifying and positive, after all! This fails, however, to take into account the ministry of Elijah and the commission given to Jeremiah, both of whose lives and callings, and others besides, must be taken as essential examples for the equipping the apostle spoke of. Both Elijah and Jeremiah delivered positive promises, as did Isaiah, but all of them also spoke words of warning, judgment and disaster should Israel fail to repent.

Fundamental to the misunderstanding under which the modern church labors with regard to prophetic ministry is a failure to comprehend the true nature and meaning of judgment. What is it? Is it punishment? Is it the expression of God's wrath? Since we have been cleansed, made holy and wear now the righteousness of Jesus, does God still judge? Or does grace make us exempt? Are we so sure that judgment is even a negative thing?

The definition of the New Testament Greek word for judgment applies to the concept of judgment in the Hebrew Old Testament as well. The word is *krino* (the verb) and *krisis* (noun). In either case its root means to cut or separate, rather than to punish. God's judgment separates the precious from the vile, the pure from the impure, the holy from the profane. In that light, should we not long for judgment and receive it as a gift?

For their failure to teach the difference between the holy and the profane, the Lord held the priests and prophets in ancient Israel accountable. "Her priests have done violence to My law and have profaned My holy things; they have made no distinction between the holy and the profane, and they have not taught the difference between the unclean and the clean" (Ezekiel 22:26). Two verses later He addressed the prophets: "Her prophets have smeared whitewash for them, seeing false visions and divining lies for them, saying, 'Thus says the Lord God,' when the Lord has not spoken" (Ezekiel 22:28).

The cross and resurrection of Jesus wash us clean from sin, but this does not inoculate us against delusion and compromise. Grace does not therefore negate the need for prophetic words that cut through the fog to discern and to declare the difference between good and evil, the clean and the unclean. God yet calls for true prophetic voices to proclaim the Lord's word where impurity and demonic deceptions have crept in. Such words have the power to expose and destroy impurity, deceiving spirits, moral compromise and theological drift. This has been and will always be a central feature of prophetic calling and a blessing to the church. Elijah and all the other biblical prophets of the Old Testament confronted the influence of Baal worship upon the people of Israel, exposing their compromises and calling them out of idolatry. This did not cease with the advent of the New Covenant.

The call to Jeremiah forms an essential part of the foundation for genuine prophetic ministry in any age. "See, I have appointed you this day over the nations and over the kingdoms, To pluck up and to break down, To destroy and to overthrow, To build and to plant" (Jeremiah 1:10). By the word of the Lord Jeremiah would uproot and destroy what did not flow from God and he would plant and build up what God wanted, whether that applied to entire nations or to ideas and practices. This is the essence of *krino* and *krisis*.

Inundated with false doctrines that undermine the very founda-
tions of our faith, and mired in growing moral compromise, today's
church stands desperately in need of the prophetic word that separates good and evil to establish purity. This is the meaning of judgment and it constitutes a primary calling for true prophetic ministry
without in any way sacrificing edification, exhortation and consolation (I Corinthians 14).

What we often think of as judgment is actually God's wrath.
Wrath is the last resort of a loving God, the devastating destruction
that falls when nothing else has worked to turn the hearts of God's
people and bring about repentance. Wrath comes as the reluctant
act of a loving Father who has patiently and desperately tried everything else to bring his beloved child out of wickedness and delusion
to no avail. Judgment is the pressure brought to bear in order to
expose good and evil and bring about repentance so that wrath can
be avoided. Wrath is needed only when judgment fails to produce the
fruit of repentance.

In either case, both judgment and wrath express the love in the
heart of God. Israel experienced many decades, even centuries, of
patient judgment and repeated warnings from prophetic voices
before wrath destroyed the nation at the hands of the Babylonians
in 586 B.C. Although wrath was certainly catastrophically painful, the
seventy years of exile in Babylon permanently cured Israel of the dis-
ease of idolatry. God did, and still does, discipline his children whom
He loves (Hebrews 12:6) in order to bring about the ultimate blessing
that can only come when purity has been established.

Understand that I would never underestimate the value of positivity. Ever in need of encouragement, we certainly need to hear
strong words of promise and uplift. We must never neglect the prophetic word, however, that separates the precious from the vile and
issues warnings of judgment and wrath if God's people fail to heed.
Can the body of Christ at last learn to hear the lonely Micaiahs who
feel out of place and sidelined by the mainstream, but whose words
would deliver us from death and destruction if we would but heed

them? How many such plumb line prophets actually find a platform to speak to thousands? To how many of them do the Christian media actually grant a voice? To what extent has the fullness of the voice of prophecy been blunted in our day?

Balance! Judgment and hope. Wrath and promise. The vile destroyed and the precious exalted! Read Jeremiah 29 or Isaiah 58 for just two prophetic passages that inject hope into the prophetic word of confrontation and judgment. Always, the pure prophetic word comes with balance, but God's people die today for lack of discernment and for a dearth of courageous prophetic voices declaring the balance of what they see, whether or not some portions are what God's people want to hear.

We desperately need a completed experience and practice of prophetic ministry in our day. As Jesus said so often, "He who has ears to hear, let him hear!"

I Corinthians 14 unpacked

I find it curious how Christians who should be functioning under grace nevertheless search the New Testament to make permanent rigid laws and rules out of statements never intended to be taken that way. Finding himself confronted with a chaotic situation in Corinth, the apostle Paul expressed the principle that whatever happens in an open service should be intelligible and accessible to the uninitiated. To accomplish this, he then gave practical guidelines appropriate to the situation and culture in Corinth.

Doesn't it make sense that the principle of order and intelligibility would require different practical applications according to and fitting for the cultures involved? Can we entertain the idea that the specifics of his instructions to the church in Corinth might not be for all of time in every situation as a set of laws, while the principle behind those specifics might stand for any culture in any age? Why would the apostle of grace and freedom be writing rigid rules to be followed in every age when, in fact, cultures and situations would change? Principles don't change. Applications of principles do change.

That being said, the relevant point for this discussion is verse 3, "But one who prophesies speaks to men for edification and exhortation and consolation." First, context reveals that this verse applies to the open meeting of the body of Christ where believers are ministering one to another and where the uninitiated might enter. Seeking to bring order and to put a boundary around this kind of mutual ministry so that no one would be hurt or confused, Paul limited the scope and spirit of words that could be safely delivered in that context. My co-author Jeremiah calls it "spontaneous prophecy".

Rules to govern this kind of prophecy would be not unlike the rules we at my church impose upon our ministry team people, many of whom *can* prophesy under the anointing, but who are not themselves prophets. We say, "No direction, correction, dates, mates or babies," so as not to set people up for hurt through prophetic words spoken by well-meaning folks who do not hold the prophetic office. They might be moving in the Holy Spirit well enough, and might even have the occasional word from God to deliver, but they are not holders of the office. We also enforce order by requiring any spontaneous word to be cleared through a staff member before being delivered. We honor and apply the principle Paul articulated with specifics that work for our culture.

By contrast, God did and does raise up in the church men and women identified as prophetic office holders. For them the rules shift, as does the calling and obligation before the Throne. Under such a calling, the scope of both calling and authority changes. Clearly, the prophet Agabus, for instance, moved well beyond the bounds of Paul's words in I Corinthians as he ministered outside the context of the kind of meeting Paul addressed.

As for positivity, I doubt that anyone in the church felt encouraged or uplifted when Agabus prophesied the coming of a great famine (Acts 11:28) or when he declared that Paul would be arrested and imprisoned if he went to Jerusalem (Acts 21:1-11). Examine the Book of Revelation. The words the Lord addressed to five of the seven churches through John's pen could as easily have come from the mouth of Elijah, Jeremiah or any one of the Old Testament prophets and yet this is New Testament prophecy. Those words confronted sin, separated the precious from the vile and called for purity in repentance. Included were words of warning if the people failed to repent. This is *krisis*, judgment at its best. John's prophecy even promised the wrath of God upon men who refused to repent. Is New Testament prophetic ministry always positive and uplifting? Hardly!

I plead for us to walk in the whole counsel of God, not just in what we feel comfortable with. Can we repent of taking, believing and allowing only those portions of the prophetic word that we like and by which we obscure and deface the fullness of the picture God paints for Himself?

Would not the contemporary church be in much better shape than it is were there a greater number of reliable prophets in our midst pointing out the error of our ways as well as speaking promise and encouragement? Unfortunately, however, when these more balanced voices speak, the body of Christ largely ignores them, relegates them to the sidelines and even criticizes them mercilessly. Thus the benefit is lost.

Down with prophetic fluff!

I, for one, tire of so-called prophetic words void of substance and deprived of passion and force. I weary of prophetic fluff spoken cheaply from the hearts of those who have yet to pay the price for character transformation into the Father's heart and the likeness of Jesus, some of whom even teach that this wilderness training is not necessary. So many prophetic "wannabes" long only to be seen by others as spiritual and powerful, or to participate in the experience they see others having or that some teacher promises to them. Prophetic ministry is not a game and it is certainly not just some great spiritual experience to be sought after. True prophetic words often come with pain and travail. For this reason, Bible scholars have called Jeremiah "the weeping prophet".

I long to see words delivered that carry the power to transform churches, people groups and nations, spoken by those who have been broken in spirit and brought into unity with the heart of the Father through character changes forged in the fire. Unfortunately, however, our too "nice" approach to ministry, born of an inadequate picture of who Jesus is in all His nature, personality and offices, bottles this up and prevents the fullness of the light from shining through. If righteousness and justice are the foundation of His throne (Psalm 97:2), then does judgment not become mandatory? And would not a loving God then send prophets to deliver us from impurity and warn us of both judgment and wrath?

Had Jehoshaphat and Ahab listened to Micaiah, they could have avoided defeat and saved Ahab's life. True prophetic ministry in our day carries the same potential to deliver us from evil, to warn us and to guide us successfully through storms and difficult days.

Stuck in the priestly function

Foundational to all of this lies the issue of whether or not Jesus remains the judge and what that means for our own ministries. Isn't it time that we recognized the fullness of who He is and applied that to ministry? We tend to focus on Jesus the high priest of our confession while we ignore or simply miss the judicial Jesus. This leads us to hear only priestly words that minister love and compassion while deafening us to words that reflect the judicial side of our Lord's nature.

He was Jesus the priest when he forgave and released the woman caught in adultery (John 8), but acted as the judge in wrath when He drove the moneychangers from the temple with a homemade knotted whip (Matthew 21:12 et al). He was Jesus the priest as He taught the Sermon on the Mount (Matthew 5-7), but Jesus the judge when confronted the Pharisees and called them snakes, hypocrites and white-washed tombs fathered by the devil. He was Jesus the priest when He healed the blind and lame and raised the dead, but He was Jesus the judge when He said of the cities that would reject His kingdom message, "Whoever does not receive you, nor heed your words, as you go out of that house or that city, shake the dust off your feet. Truly I say to you, it will be more tolerable for the land of Sodom and Gomorrah in the day of judgment than for that city" (Matthew 10:14-15).

The apostle Paul wrote Timothy to speak of, "Christ Jesus, who is to judge the living and the dead, and by His appearing in His kingdom." Jesus the judge taught:

> You will know them by their fruits. Grapes are not gathered from thorn bushes nor figs from thistles, are they? So every good tree bears good fruit, but the bad tree bears bad fruit. A good tree cannot produce bad fruit, nor can a bad tree produce good fruit. Every tree that does not bear good fruit is cut down and thrown into the fire. So then, you will know them by their fruits. Not everyone who says to Me, "Lord, Lord," will enter the kingdom of heaven, but he who does the will of My Father who is in heaven will enter. Many will say to Me on that day, "Lord, Lord, did we not prophesy in Your name, and in Your name cast out demons, and in Your name perform many miracles?" And then I will declare to them, "I never knew you; depart from Me, you who practice lawlessness" (Matthew 7:16-23).

Then, in the very next chapter, Jesus the merciful priest stretched out His hand to touch and heal a leper. Is Jesus still the judge? True prophetic voices must balance the priestly nature of our Lord with the judicial side of who He is. We carry an obligation to reveal the whole nature of the One for whom we speak, lest, through the filter of our own hearts, unwilling to hear the fullness, we prophecy falsely. "The testimony of Jesus is the spirit of prophecy" (Revelation 19:10). Will we represent and speak for all that He is, or only those aspects of His nature with which we are comfortable?

Jezebel sought to kill Elijah for his opposition to the intrusion the spirit of Baal into the lives of the people of God. Because Micaiah spoke what the kings did not want to hear, they cast him into prison and fed him on bread and water. Jeremiah found himself at the bottom of a well. I guarantee that if Hananiah, who disagreed with Jeremiah concerning the fate of Israel, were alive today, he'd sell more books and draw greater crowds than Jeremiah ever would. "'Then Hananiah the prophet took the yoke from the neck of Jeremiah the prophet and broke it. Hananiah spoke in the presence of all the people, saying, "Thus says the Lord, 'Even so will I break within two full years the yoke of Nebuchadnezzar king of Babylon from the neck of all the nations'" (Jeremiah 28:10-11). In the end, Hananiah's false word, regardless of how popular it was, cost him his life (Jeremiah 28:16-17).

Is Jesus still the judge? Most certainly. Is that a negative? Most certainly not. Let the faithful Micaiahs arise with the courage to deliver not just the pleasant words of promise from the heart of God, but the fullness of the Father, Savior, Priest, Healer, King and Judge.

6
Accountability
(R. Loren Sandford)

CLEARLY, I CORINTHIANS 14:29 calls for mechanisms of accountability in prophetic ministry, especially in an age when we are fresh out of men the like of Elijah, Isaiah, Jeremiah and company. "Let two or three prophets speak, and let the others pass judgment." But where do we find any such effective mechanisms of check and balance in the body of Christ today? Where is the accountability for inaccurate and wrong words given, much less a structure for testing those words before they're given? How many prophetic ministers operate independently, outside the structures of the local church where God-ordained checks and balances can operate?

Too many prophetic people whose gifts might be genuine reject the correction that would come through relationships in the local church. They complain that pastors and people don't understand them and even reject their words. Too often this is the case because of two dynamics crashing into one another.

First, untrained and unbroken people with prophetic gifts often tend to be obnoxious and arrogant in their presentation, failing to understand that their place lies in submission to the authorities God has established in the local church. They have yet to embrace the kind of humility and brokenness that win them favor with both God and man.

"The tongue of the wise makes knowledge acceptable..." (Proverbs 15:2). Wise pastors can help such young prophetic voices learn how better to communicate, but, more importantly, knowledge can come from study, but real wisdom comes only from suffering. The erstwhile prophet who has not yet embraced the wilderness of correction and rebuke, and allowed it to shape his or her character, will be a loose cannon on the Lord's deck, unnecessarily mistrusted and unreceived by the very ones they're called to benefit.

Second, it is true that most pastors don't understand prophetic people, much less the true function and purpose of prophetic ministry. They tend either to reject prophetic people and their ministry outright, rather than be part of shepherding them into maturity, or they seek to use them inappropriately to build up their ministries. Rare is the pastor who truly understands and wisely deals with prophetic ministry and prophetic people under his or her care.

I have often joked that true prophetic people are usually two french-fries short of a Happy Meal. Serious discipling is needed. In order to minister effectively to prophetic people, pastors must study to understand both the true nature of prophetic ministry and the personality profile of the prophetic people they have been called to shepherd. For an in depth examination of this particular subject and the accountability it can bring, I suggest my book, *Understanding Prophetic People*.

Perhaps more importantly, the emerging Micaiah Company will be what I call "pastoral prophets". For much too long we have had major prophetic ministries operating independently, outside the structures of the local church and answering only to themselves. At least two disadvantages result from this. The first is that such ministries are too often removed from any kind of God-ordained corrective structure. These ministries incorporate independently and have administrative boards of directors, but it is too easy to fill such boards with those chosen to support by agreement or to deal with mere financial accountability, rather than provide spiritual balance.

The second problem develops as the prophet at the top of the independent ministry becomes too detached from the actual flock of God. Many years ago, John Wimber chastised a group of Vineyard pastors gathered for a conference for not being connected enough to those they led, suggesting that a true shepherd should smell like his sheep. The only way to pick up sheep scent is to hang out with them. True New Testament prophetic people carrying the heart of Father God humble themselves to come under the church to lift it as they walk in covenant relationship with its Lord and its people.

It used to be said that prophets make poor pastors because of temperament and personality traits common to them. No longer. God has shifted the paradigm. Prophetic people – people of the Micaiah Company - must have the heart of the Shepherd. We are going to see increasing numbers of prophetic people in the Micaiah Company pastoring local churches even as they carry the prophetic office. In doing so, they will better and more accurately communicate the heart of the Father. In that spirit, people will hear them more readily and take their words more deeply to heart.

A generational shift

An older generation of prophetic leaders, operating under the older paradigm of the independently incorporated ministry, has been passing away or retiring. A new generation of younger voices, given to the church, involved in it, submitted to it and caring for it is now emerging. They have more concern for caring than for prophesying. Their hearts burn for intimacy with God and for His ways more than for standing before audiences to wow them with their gifting. Representing Jesus with fullness and accuracy will mean more to them than building great ministries that bear their own names.

As this shift progresses, and an older generation with an older paradigm dies off, a remnant of seasoned older prophets will remain to father and mentor the rising generation. They are themselves part of the Micaiah Company and they carry the same heart. Their calling is an Elijah calling, to train and release a company of Elishas, spiritual sons and daughters whose gifts and anointing actually exceed their own. Gifting and anointing need the seasoned wisdom of those who've gone before to make them stable and effective. Thus the hearts of the fathers are restored to the children and the children to the fathers (Malachi 4:5-6) in these last days leading to the return of the Lord.

In Exodus 33:12 God assured Moses that he had found favor in God's sight. Moses' response illustrates the heart of the emerging Micaiah Company. "Now therefore, I pray You, if I have found favor in Your sight, let me know Your ways that I may know You, so that I may find favor in Your sight" (Exodus 33:13). More concerned with absorbing the character of God as his own than with leading a great company of people in power, Moses asked God for that which would make him a safe and reliable leader, worthy of the Lord's trust. Let God's ways be our ways at the level of real life, both inwardly and in our dealings with others. While we may gather men and women of wisdom around us for check and for balance, the ultimate account-ability flows from God Himself and rests upon godly character forged in the wilderness and steeped in humility.

When prophetic words fail

We so desperately long for words from God concerning our destinies, our lives and our hopes for our nation and the world, that when a prophetic word proves to be inaccurate and fails to come to pass, we tend either to ignore it or make attempts at "stretch-to-fit". I call it "rubber prophecy". We say that it was only symbolic or that it wasn't time or – if the prophecy was a warning of a disaster to come – we say that, because people prayed, it didn't happen. That may be true sometimes, but most often it's simply a dodge. The list of justifica-tions and excuses we use to avoid facing the fact that the prophecy was false is a long one. Worse, we continue to listen to prophets whose words have been consistently inaccurate, so long as the words they give continue to excite our emotions.

The tragedy here is that when we do this, when we fail to look at fruit and hold prophetic people accountable, when we fail to honestly face the fact of failure, we cheat ourselves and prophetic people of the opportunity to examine what went wrong and to learn from it. God's people need to tell us when we're wrong and pastors need to lovingly help us work through the reasons why it went wrong. What was the pollution, brokenness, immaturity or fleshly motivation that caused him or her to hear that inaccurate word and to believe it was the voice of God?

Without accountability and a humble willingness to submit to it, how can we learn and grow? By failing to hold our prophetic people accountable, providing structures for balance and correction, we therefore set them up for continued failure and we enable the ongoing debacle that is so much of the prophetic movement today.

My story
I have lived with prophetic ministry all my life. I was seven years old in 1958 when my father and mother received the baptism in the Holy Spirit and began to walk in the things of the Spirit. Thereafter, because my father had always been the mystical type, we lived day to day in a kind of prophetic soup that seemed like normal life to me. My prophetic father actually dreamed the assassination of President Kennedy before it happened. Visions, dreams and accounts of translations to heaven were the stuff of daily conversation over breakfast. As a child I knew nothing else and thought everyone lived like this. I didn't know how different we were.

Before long, my father became a leader in pioneering prophetic ministry internationally across the Charismatic Movement. There isn't much, therefore, that I haven't seen.

That being said, somewhat less than 10% of anything prophesied over my own life and ministry has actually come to any measure of fulfillment in any form, and I have received prophetic words from the very top names in the prophetic movement. For the sake of respect and honor, I refuse to name names, but I must nevertheless tell a few stories. Those who have prophesied these things over my life have been people whose commitment to the Lord and whose passion for him I deeply respect. Some of them have led many more people to Jesus than I have ever touched or ever will, and I will not dishonor them if I can possibly avoid doing so.

It was 1988 at the height of the prophetic frenzy then under way in the Charismatic wing of the body of Christ. Perhaps 1000 pastors had gathered for a conference in the affiliation I was then part of. One name stood out from the pack in those days as the leading prophetic voice for that time. It was commonly and confidently stated that his words never fell to the ground. Everyone I knew stood in awe of his prophetic gift.

Like so many others, I sat with tense anticipation in the audience, hoping to be called out to receive a word of hope for my life and ministry during a very difficult season, and then it happened. He called me out of the crowd and prophesied that a great restoration of marriages would come to pass in my church and that through that church I would leave a legacy for my children. Neither of these things ever happened. In fact, a key leadership couple divorced rather catastrophically shortly after that and nearly shattered the congregation. Three years later, the Lord clearly called me out of that church after a series of crises that began with the failure of that key couple. Shortly after I had moved on, the church closed. That was the beginning of my cynicism, not about prophetic ministry itself, but about the current prophetic movement.

In 1992, after leaving an associate position I had taken with a megachurch, I planted my current congregation, New Song Church and Ministries, under a hail of gunfire and slander directed rather personally at me. To say that the dirt directed at me was wounding would be a gross understatement. At the time, it cost me friends and affiliations in a variety of places and sent me into a long and deep depression, even as I fought to found and inspire the new congregation.

That fall, a couple of months into the planting of the church, my associate pastor, his wife, my parents, my wife and I held a small weekday retreat with one of the top recognized prophetic voices in the nation who had become a close friend to my father and mother.

She knew how wounded I was and prophesied that New Song would become so large that even the senior pastor of the church I had left – and who had spoken such vile things of me – would have to admit it was God. Twenty-five long years later, not a word of that prophecy has come anywhere near fulfillment, although New Song is a stable and strong congregation, a pretty wonderful congregation to be part of. God shows up consistently and His presence is always felt. The prophecy, however, fell to the ground.

Ten years later, the same prophetic leader who prophesied to me in that private retreat, called me out of a crowd of pastors gathered for a breakfast meeting to prophesy publicly that the Lord was going to give my congregation a new building, bigger, visible and with lots of parking for the multitudes who would come for the miracle center. At that time our building was on the market and we were hoping to move to a more advantageous location after the sale. Now fourteen years later we remain stuck in the same facility in an unattractive neighborhood with half the parking needed to service our seating capacity, while the rise in property values in our city has made moving ever more impossible. That prophetic person simply tuned into my deep desire to move and reflected it back as a word from God. And, while we've seen miracles over the years, never has it been anything like what she prophesied.

Recently, I pulled out of my files a set of prophetic words my wife and I received at a by-invitation-only gathering of prophetic people just a few years ago. I highly respect the one who convened this meeting and I am in no way impugning the part he contributed to the list of prophecies. Although his contribution was short on any real specifics, it was not inaccurate. In light of the passage of time, however, the others who prophesied at the meeting were clearly and simply "off" in virtually everything.

In 2012 two highly regarded prophets from a very well-known contemporary movement prophesied over my wife, my son and me at a pastors' gathering. For the sake of brevity, I won't list all that they said, but not a word of what they prophesied came to pass, in spite of the fact that it felt so much like God. In addition to other specifics, the word was that the next two years would be years of intense preparation and that 2014 would be a really big deal for us as a ministry. They foresaw a time of breakthrough and expansion. In reality, 2014 was the worst year of struggle and loss we had experienced in a number of years. The specifics of those prophetic words were wrong, no matter what way you might try to stretch them, as well as the timeline prophesied. Worse, what actually came to pass was the very opposite of the blessing they had proclaimed.

Am I bitter about all this? Not at all. Rather, I am deeply concerned and grieved because stories similar to mine abound. I hear them month by month much more often than I hear of prophetic words fulfilled, and I see the hurt and disappointment in too many lives touched by failed prophecies. In many of these folks, bitterness has taken root and now colors their outlook on the Lord, the body of Christ and certainly their attitude toward prophetic ministry in general. What began as hope, ended in despair and loss of hope.

To be fair, there have been some accurate prophetic words spoken concerning my life and ministry over the years, although few and far between. The most accurate words fulfilled over time came not from some superstar on the platform or from a famous recognized leader, but from a prophetic team of nobodies in a private meeting in Toronto in the second year of the outpouring there. One could wonder whether some lesson ought to be drawn from that.

In any case, the prophetic movement stands desperately in need of some course corrections. Accountability must be one element. Real prophetic people with a true desire to reflect the heart of the Father won't wait for it to come to them. They'll seek it out.

Some principles of accountability

In 2012 or 2013 I was privileged to be part of compiling a document with a very long title: *Biblical Principles Concerning Ethics and Protocols*

Relating to New Testament Prophetic Ministry. John Paul Jackson and Marc Dupont conceived of and spearheaded the effort. In addition to John Paul Jackson, Marc Dupont and me, the team included James Goll, Bobby Connor and my father, John Sandford. Because the resulting document grew to be quite long, I'll cite only some pertinent portions here.

We began by affirming the absolute truth of the written Word of God and we bound ourselves to being tested by it in all things. We recognized that speaking a word supposedly from God constitutes a serious responsibility and that nothing less than aspiring to 100% accuracy would be acceptable. We committed to take certain actions when we were shown to be wrong. We would, "...take steps to acknowledge, repent and make restitution for my error in a prophecy or its delivery, in a manner appropriate to correct the error and the reason for the error." We went further than this. We committed to full repentance and to a procedure to rectify the harm done. This included the following:

A. An apology. If I gave the prophecy to a private party, my apology must be to that party. If the prophecy was given to a group such as a church or the public, the apology must be given to that group.

B. Biblical repentance does not mean saying, "I'm sorry" only to God, but also to those I have hurt. Most importantly, I must communicate that I am deeply concerned about the harm I have done or the hurt I have inflicted, and I will do whatever else is needed to help heal the wounds I have caused.

C. With the help of wise counsel, I will seek to find if there is anything in my heart that caused this error, and deal with it through confession, repentance and action.

D. I commit to continuing in accountability to a safe and loving authority whom I believe will support me and help me walk in integrity. I will not remove myself from this process even if painful to me and/or it seems that those to whom I am accountable are not treating me fairly.

E. I believe there are consequences to all actions. If my error is particularly serious or repeated, I will be willing to take time off from prophetic ministry until I and those in authority over me have discerned that I am ready to resume ministry.

The document states:

Understanding a prophetic word is vital to its implementation. Therefore, I commit to being open to discuss, with appropriate leaders within the Body of Christ, the prophetic words I receive and interpretations of those words. I will endeavor to do so because prophetic gifts are given to serve the people, not to promote the one who prophesies.

This one was essential:

I commit to having an accountability group in place to whom I will hold my lifestyle, marriage and ministry accountable.

Our prayer was that this document would find wide distribution and that many itinerant prophetic ministers and others with prophetic gifts and callings would commit to the principles contained in it. To date, should you wish to read the document in its entirety, simply run a Google search on the title. Multiple references will result.

Taking the Lord's name in vain

I wonder how many of us truly understand the danger of speaking carelessly in the Lord's name when the Lord has not spoken? How many of us realize that it's not about exercising our gifts, and certainly not about being recognized for them? We're messing with people's lives and, if we get it wrong, we've not only damaged those God loves, but we've misrepresented God Himself!

"You shall not take the name of the Lord your God in vain, for the Lord will not leave him unpunished who takes His name in vain"

(Exodus 20:7). This is not primarily about swearing! To speak in some-one's name is to speak as and for that person. The reference there-fore points to how God's discipline falls when we represent our words as coming from Him when He has not actually spoken. As important as the words themselves is the spirit in which they are spoken. Is His true nature communicated? Given my personal experience and the experience of multitudes of others, you have to know that many peo-ple irresponsibly speak in the Lord's name when He has not spoken and they are not being held accountable in the church for crossing that line. God takes this seriously! Prophetic ministry is not a game. It is rather the gravest of responsibilities.

Faulty training

In general, we take prophetic ministry much too lightly while we cheaply franchise it to any and all. Again and again I hear pastoral leaders and big "names" carelessly encouraging literally everyone to prophesy. Is that really what God wants? Is this really something authorized and encouraged in the biblical record? If so, then why was Micaiah outnumbered 400 to one? The result of this loose dis-semination of empowerment to speak prophetically might look and feel like glory at the moment in the heat of an anointed meet-ing, but later it results in chaos and harm. Yes, God can and some-times does prophesy through the least of us, but the reliable pro-phetic person remains a rarity. Those with a true prophetic calling undergo rigorous training, seasoning and an extended wilderness of crushing and breaking for character formation before ever being allowed to speak in the Lord's name in a manner to be recognized as authoritative.

And yet, conferences are held at which everyone present is told that they can prophesy and they are given what passes as simple tools to enable them to do it. This is often followed by a so-called acti-vation or impartation. What should begin with character formation and proceed to method or approach then begins with the method or approach at the expense of character training. This misses the scriptural pattern and can fill the immature with unwarranted and dangerous delusions of grandeur. To give credit where credit is due, I will always remember listening gratefully to John Paul Jackson's seminar, *The Art of Hearing God*, a number of years ago. Nearly the entire course focused on character issues, holiness and brokenness before God.

Elijah called Elisha to follow him, appointed him his successor and imparted to him the double portion of his mantle. Ignorance of Bible culture leads to misunderstanding of this passing of the mantle, and therefore to error in practice as it leaves out the essential relational component.

Sonship in humility

In Bible times, if a man had two sons, he would divide his inheritance three ways. The eldest son received two portions while the younger son received one. As the flaming chariot caught Elijah up to heaven, Elisha cried out, "My father, my father, the chariots of Israel and its horsemen!" First, in light of the culture of the day, understand that when Elisha asked for the double portion of Elijah's mantle, he was not asking for twice as much. Elijah would not have had that to give because he could not impart more than he had been given. Second, in Scripture, impartation happens in the context of an intimate relationship between a spiritual father and a spiritual son. Not cheap! Not easy! Not done in a just a day or two at a conference! In reality, Elisha requested not twice as much, but the double portion of an inheritance that rightly belonged to the firstborn or primary son of his father!

A New Testament example would be Paul's relationship with Timothy. "I remind you to kindle afresh the gift of God which is in you through the laying on of my hands" (II Timothy 1:6). Misapplying this verse, ministries have been built around cheap so-called impartations of spiritual gifts in conference settings where no real relationship exists between the teacher and the conference attendees. Notice that Paul's relationship with Timothy was that of a spiritual father to a spiritual son. Paul addressed the letter we call II Timothy to "Timothy *my beloved son*" (1:2).

For such a relationship to exist, a price must be paid. It requires submission over a period of time to one more mature in the ministry. It requires humility in laying aside pride to serve the older master. This brings us to perhaps the most important element in a prophet's training.

Wilderness training

Again and again in Scripture you see major leaders undergoing a wilderness experience, an extended season – or multiple seasons – of crushing, humbling and breaking for character formation. For example, you find this experience embedded in a curious statement made concerning Elisha. King Jehoshaphat needed a word from God concerning a coming battle and said this: "'Is there not a prophet of the Lord here, that we may inquire of the Lord by him?' And one of the king of Israel's servants answered and said, 'Elisha the son of Shaphat is here, who used to pour water on the hands of Elijah'" (II Kings 3:11).

In the culture of Bible times this was a woman's work. For a man to perform this task would have been profoundly shattering to his ego, the deepest of humiliations. Long before Elisha could be allowed to prophesy, he had to learn to serve in the most humbling ways. He had to learn first what he could not do before he could learn what he could do. Without such brokenness and humility, he could never have safely administered the prophetic word. How many today would choose to humble themselves in such a fashion? On a lesser scale, in the movie, *The Karate Kid,* before Daniel San could learn karate from Mr. Miyagi, he had first to sand the floor in humble service to his sensei, not knowing or understanding that by sanding the floor he was actually learning karate. Perhaps it's time for erstwhile prophetic people to learn to, "Sand the floor!" and know that in humble service they are actually learning the heart of our Lord to equip them for the calling.

Before taking the Promised Land, Israel wandered forty years in the dry desert wilderness while a faithless generation died off. When the character of the nation had been sufficiently formed and purified in the heat of that wilderness, they entered the land as conquerors.

David underwent many years in the wilderness after being anointed king before being allowed to actually become king. He led a ragtag gang of social rejects in exile while being hunted by Saul, the very king he had desired only to serve. This season of humiliation, crushing and breaking for character formation prepared him to become Israel's finest king, the man after God's own heart.

Jesus Himself spent forty days and nights in the wilderness, sent there by the Holy Spirit in order to be tempted by the devil. There, in that time of testing and suffering, He faced very real temptation, solidified His sense of identity, and made the decisions for obedience that qualified Him to become the Messiah and save us all.

The apostle Paul spent fourteen years sidelined in Tarsus making tents after his initial success in Damascus before Barnabas sent for him to come to Antioch. Can you imagine how that felt to a man as gifted and driven as Paul?

Wilderness destroys fleshly ambition. It wrecks the need to be seen. It teaches humility in ways that none of us can teach ourselves, destroying every fleshly confidence in self until nothing remains but a purified hunger for the Lord Himself. Wilderness exposes and destroys brokenness. It leaves in its wake a purified hunger just to be with Jesus and a sense of satisfaction that obedience is its own reward, regardless of fleshly measures of success by the world's standard.

You see it in David's poetry in Psalm 63:1-2, "O God, You are my God; I shall seek You earnestly; My soul thirsts for You, my flesh yearns for You, In a dry and weary land where there is no water. Thus I have seen You in the sanctuary, To see Your power and Your glory." When deprived of everything else – fruit from ministry, blessing in life, success on the world's terms, even the sense of the presence of

God - a purified hunger for the Lord takes root until the revelation of who He is becomes all that matters.

Until that happens, no matter how gifted the erstwhile prophet might be, he or she will substitute for the presence of God the rush that comes from success and the affirmations that flow from men and women admiring and being awed by the gifting. Untrained and unbroken, he or she will never know the difference. Polluted prophecies will result, as will abusive or off-base ministry practices. People will be hurt and God will be misrepresented.

In *Understanding Prophetic People* I've written extensively on the wilderness and the dark night of the soul, supporting it carefully from Scripture. For deeper understanding, please get and read that book. For now, understand that misfocused, bad or inaccurate prophetic ministry happens when we neglect to tell people about the wilderness experience. Things go wrong when we deploy prophetic people and grant the platform before wilderness seasoning has done its work.

Instead of preparing hearts for necessary suffering and enabling them to embrace it for redemption and change, we teach that all suffering is of the devil and not of God. Confusion then reigns when the wilderness descends. If the Holy Spirit led Jesus into forty days of fellowship with Satan while starving Himself, what makes us think that we who are sinful should escape a similar testing?

Remember Peter's statement that, "he who has suffered in the flesh has ceased from sin" (I Peter 4:1). Redemptive suffering occupies an essential place in the training of a prophet. "And we know that God causes all things to work together for good to those who love God, to those who are called according to His purpose. For those whom He foreknew, He also predestined to become conformed to the image of His Son, so that He would be the firstborn among many brethren" (Romans 8:28-29). To speak the word of God we must carry the heart and character of God.

Prophecy when cheaply franchised produces cheap results and poor fruit. It's time we told the truth.

7

Are There Any Other Prophets?

(Jeremiah Johnson)

IN 1 KINGS 22, Ahab the King of Israel asks Jehoshaphat the King of Judah to enter into battle with him against the King of Aram to take over Ramoth-Gilead. King Jehoshaphat sets the terms of agreement to partner with King Ahab in verse five as he says, "inquire first for the word of the Lord." King Ahab responds by quickly by calling upon his 400 prophets and receives his answer. They say, "Go into battle, for the Lord will deliver Ramoth-Gilead into your hands." Appearing to be unsatisfied, King Jehoshaphat says, "are there any other prophets to inquire of for the word of the Lord?" King Ahab reluctantly says that there is one other prophet whose name is Micaiah, but Ahab dislikes him because he has not given favorable prophecies to Ahab in the past.

As Micaiah is summoned by a messenger from the king, he is warned to give an acceptable prophecy, but Micaiah says that he will speak only what the Lord tells him to speak. Standing before Ahab and Jehoshaphat, Micaiah at first delivers a similar prophecy to his prophetic contemporaries, prophesying that the kings should go to battle, but when he is pressed further by Ahab to speak only the truth of what the Lord has spoken to him, Micaiah declares that he saw a vision where God asks the question, "who will entice Ahab to go into battle that he may perish?" Micaiah then says that he saw a lying spirit step forward and fill the mouths of Ahab's 400 prophets with lies. Infuriated, Ahab sentences Micaiah to prison until he returns from battle. Just as Micaiah prophesied, King Ahab enters into battle and is fatally wounded by the army of Aram.

I believe that just as King Jehoshaphat asked King Ahab if there were "any other prophets" to inquire of for the word of the Lord, so that same heart's desire is being magnified and echoed all across America by increasing numbers of saints and leaders. "Are there any other prophets?" has become the responsive heart cry of a growing group of people heartbroken over what much of the contemporary prophetic movement is claiming that God is saying. They believe that there must be real prophets in the land who will unashamedly deliver the word of the Lord.

Just as in the days of Micaiah where he alone represented a small company of voices in the land that stood opposed to Ahab's 400 prophets, so this same scenario is being played out in America today. I believe there is a Micaiah Company that has been largely hidden and reserved for such a time as this. It is imperative, however, that we recognize the current trends in the prophetic movement so that we might welcome many of these voices whom God has been forging in secret.

Two Prophetic Companies

Two very distinct companies are emerging from the current prophetic movement that mirror the situation in the days of Micaiah. The first company is the "politically correct company". This group is fueled by an embrace of spontaneous prophecy that is purely encouraging, uplifting, and "feel good". This style of prophecy thrives on telling people what they want to hear. Any prophetic words of warning, rebuke, or correction are categorically rejected by those in this pro- phetic camp while individuals like Micaiah who release these types of words are labeled wounded, rebellious, critical, and oftentimes arrogant. The goal of politically correct prophecy is to keep everyone happy and believing that God is in a good mood all the time.

I call the second emerging company the "prophetically correct" company. While this prophetic company embraces spontaneous prophecy, revelatory prophetic words that root out, pull down, destroy, and overthrow are welcomed and received by this group. What the politically correct camp calls "critical", the prophetically correct camp calls "biblical". The goal of the prophetically correct camp is to deliver the word and heart of the Lord, whether the people like it or not. In the same spirit as Micaiah, this company's allegiance is found in their commitment to "prophesy only what the Lord says" regardless of how well it is received.

As in the days of Micaiah, one of the core issues that separate these two prophetic companies in America is the definition of what exactly characterizes authentic prophets. What did Micaiah understand about the nature of Yahweh that the 400 prophets did not?

The Nature of Prophets

We must understand that the nature of the gift of prophecy (available to all believers) is COMPLETELY different than the nature of the ministry of the prophet (only some are called). The current politically correct camp seems to embrace only the gift of prophecy that brings very general encouragement, strength, and comfort.

They categorically reject and simply do not understand the nature of authentic prophets as found in Jeremiah 1:10. When those called as true prophets of God start rooting out, pulling down, destroying, and throwing down carnality, structures, practices, movements, men, and traditions that oppose the purposes and plans of God, the politically correct camp labels them, "critical", "negative", wounded" and "rebellious" when they are actually fulfilling their mandate (4 parts negative, 2 parts positive)! Yes, prophets of God are absolutely called to build, plant and move in the nature of the *gift* of prophecy (encouragement, strength, and comfort), but they WILL NOT do so if they discern carnality, structures, and foundations that are not built upon the person of Jesus Christ. This Micaiah Company will expose, confront, tear down, uproot and call out issues and people that oppose the desires of God.

I firmly believe that the *gift* of prophecy, as opposed to the prophetic office, has become so exalted in the contemporary prophetic movement, and overall prophetic ministry so watered down, that we can't even recognize authentic prophets anymore. We do not know how to rejoice and celebrate the Micaiah Company and the nature of the call on their lives. And oh, how we desperately need to make room for them in our movements and in the American church today.

Biblical History
Throughout biblical history, one of the primary issues God had with false prophets was that they led the people into believing that they were at peace with God when in fact they were not. In essence, nowhere in Scripture does God promise peace and prosperity to a nation, tribe, or people who do not walk according to His counsel because to fail to do so violates His character and nature. For an individual to prophesy that God is going to bless a nation that has turned its back on Him is to invoke the judgment of Almighty God. For Micaiah to tell Ahab that he would have victory in battle when in fact that was not what God was saying would have been for Micaiah to invite the judgment of the Almighty upon His life. For the politically correct camp in America to continue to promise that blessing and peace are coming to our nation as we legalize homosexual marriage, accelerate the murder of over 50 million innocent babies, and a slew of other injustices is to invoke the judgment of Almighty God.

False and True Prophets in America
False prophets declare peace, blessing, and prosperity to nations and leaders living in sin. True prophets of God declare repentance, reform, and impending judgment to nations and leaders living in sin. If the United States of America is currently and unashamedly legislating wickedness and immorality on an unprecedented level like never

before, why is it so hard for the people of God to discern who the false prophets are and who the true prophets of God are?

The answer is again found in Jeremiah 5:31 as the prophet says, "The prophets prophesy falsely, the priests rule by their own authority and MY PEOPLE LOVE IT SO". In other words, people generally love false prophecy! They crave false prophets who tickle their ears with false hopes of soulish destiny and financial prosperity. False prophets draw the largest crowds and have the most popularity in America.

I caution you to NOT be surprised in the United States of America as the people of God cry out for and welcome false prophets who will promise increasing blessing, peace, and prosperity in the coming days. If this nation does not repent of her sins on a mass scale, revival and awakening will never occur and the judgment of God will be released in ever increasing measure. This is not doomsday prophecy, this is the authority of God's Word. There has never been a nation in biblical history that has turned their back on God and not reaped the consequences for their disobedience. It doesn't matter who prophesies what and especially how popular they are. Stop listening to the words of men and search the Scriptures for TRUTH.

You can prophesy all the hope you want for America, but our only hope is found in repentance. You can prophesy all the healing you want for America, but our only hope is found in repentance. You can prophesy all the revival and awakening you want for America, but none of that will happen without repentance.

The Days of Ezekiel

Ezekiel cried out against false prophets in his day and said:

> Therefore, this is what the Sovereign Lord says: Because what you say is false and your visions are a lie, I will stand against you, says the Sovereign Lord. I will raise my fist against all the prophets who see false visions and make lying predictions, and they will be banished from the

community of Israel. I will blot their names from Israel's record books, and they will never again set foot in their own land. Then you will know that I am the Sovereign Lord. This will happen because these evil prophets deceive my people by saying, "All is peaceful" when there is no peace at all! It's as if the people have built a flimsy wall, and these prophets are trying to reinforce it by covering it with whitewash! (Ezekiel 13:8-10)

The Days of Jeremiah

On numerous occasions Jeremiah cried out against the false prophets who opposed him in his days as he said:

This is what the Lord of Heaven's Armies says to his people: "Do not listen to these prophets when they prophesy to you, filling you with futile hopes. They are making up everything they say. They do not speak for the Lord! They keep saying to those who despise my word, 'Don't worry! The Lord says you will have peace!' And to those who stubbornly follow their own desires, they say, 'No harm will come your way!'" (Jeremiah 23: 16-17)

What did Micaiah, Ezekiel, and Jeremiah understand about the character and nature of God that their prophetic contemporaries did not? What does the prophetically correct company in America understand about who God is that the politically correct company does not? I believe it lies in a revelation of the justice of God and how He chooses to deal with humanity according to how they respond to His truth.

The Word of God

In both the Old and New Covenants, it is clear that God chooses to deal with His people according to how they respond to His truth. Sixteen times in the Old Testament, love and truth are wrapped together in a bundle. If the people responded to God in repentance and truth, He kept his love for thousands of generations and forgave their iniquity, transgressions, and sins. (Exodus 34:7). God's lovingkindness in the Old Testament was reserved for those who responded rightly to His truth. But to those who refused His truth, they also forsook His love and were not left unpunished. (Exodus 20:5)

In the New Covenant, it is absolutely clear that Jesus Christ has come and borne the wrath of God upon the cross for our sins (Romans 5:8). All those who have put their faith in the Son of God will be spared from eternal judgment. This is the good news of the gospel! Having said that, God will release another type of judgment upon believers in the form of His discipline as He seeks to conform them into His likeness. In both 1 Corinthians 11 and Revelation 3, the word discipline is translated as "judgement" in the original Greek.

In other words, as New Covenant believers, Jesus still deals with us according to how we respond to His truth. If we commit sin and harden our hearts to His voice, He will chastise and discipline us because He loves us.

Distorted Love
One of the great errors or mistakes that many in the contemporary prophetic movement currently make and teach is that the judgment of God is not New Covenant. If you are referring to judgment as wrath in the form of eternal judgment, then yes, the blood of Jesus covers us. But if you are talking about *krisis* judgment that separates the precious from the vile, then, no, we are not spared from these dealings of God. We must distinguish the different types of judgment so that we do not lead people astray into false doctrine.

If God is still dealing with believers according to how they respond to His truth, then it is imperative that we define love. The discipline of God is a manifestation of His great love for us. It is completely biblical for a prophet of God under the New Covenant to rebuke and correct a believer or a church leader with regard to their sin. Does it need to be done in brokenness and with love? Absolutely! But remember, the politically correct camp of prophets cannot stomach this truth.

They say that all prophecy must be positive, encouraging, and uplifting. Even worse, when a prophet of God begins to prophesy words of correction and rebuke to the body of Christ for how they have failed to uphold a standard of righteousness in the land, we tell them to be quiet.

I have been in several meetings where major voices in the contemporary prophetic movement have told young prophets on no uncertain terms to stop calling out the sin of America, the church and its shepherds. "We are living under a New Covenant" they say. Meanwhile, deception and a silencing of the word of the Lord is established in the prophetic movement.

Here Come the Prophets

I do believe that there are "other prophets" that are about to come out of hiding and many of them will not be politically correct. Just as Micaiah stood opposed to 400 prophets in his day, so these "other prophets" will often release prophetic words that will contradict what their contemporaries are saying. This Micaiah Company will not turn a blind eye to the sin of America, the body of Christ, or its people. They will release the discipline and chastisement of the Lord. To those who have eyes to see and ears to hear, their words will be one of the greatest acts of love and blessing that the American Church has ever known.

The Micaiah Company will continually call for repentance, reform, and revival. Are you listening to the prophetically correct camp in America or are you listening to the politically correct camp in America? Your answer to this question will be directly connected to whether or not you believe that God deals with His people according to how they respond to His truth. How should God respond to a nation that has taken prayer out of school, legalized gay marriage and aborted millions of innocent babies? How should God deal with His body who have chosen to remain silent on these issues when we should be speaking out?

We can talk about the goodness and love of God all that we want, but when His love starts manifesting as severe discipline and chastisement, let's embrace it. When the Micaiah Company starts trumpeting the call for repentance and rebuking and correcting the body of Christ, let's rejoice! Let us thank God that He loves us too much to leave us the way that He found us. To continue to prophesy to saints that God is at peace with them when they are living in immorality and sin is to blaspheme the Holy Spirit. We must accurately represent who God the Father really is in this hour and I believe the Micaiah Company will not only know His kindness, but also reveal His severity.

8
Prophetic Prostitution
(Jeremiah Johnson)

"JEREMIAH, IF YOU want a good love offering tonight, I need you to prophesy to these specific people," the pastor said. He was referring to a board that he had pulled out from behind his desk in the green room with people's faces on it. In total shock, I took a deep breath and said to the Lord, "So this is what I have been waiting for, for the last ten years? I'm here at my first prophetic gathering to minister and I'm already being asked to be a prophetic prostitute?" The Holy Spirit immediately responded to me and said, "Choose life or death today, for I have sent you here to test your heart and make sure you understand how polluted the prophetic movement in America has really become."

Minutes later, I would walk out onto the stage before a room full of people hungry for prophetic words of prosperity. As I scanned the room, I began to recognize many of the people whose faces were on the board that I was shown in the green room. They wore expensive jewelry and were dressed in fine clothing. Then I noticed those in the crowd who were visibly poor and broken. They had nothing to offer but a genuine desire to connect with God and to pursue intimacy with Jesus. For the next few hours, I chose to stand up those in the meeting who I believed were hurting and less fortunate and ministered the Father's love and destiny over their lives. It was one of the most powerful meetings that I have ever been in, but I left that night with-out a love offering or a single word from the pastor.

Manipulating messengers
I can only imagine how Micaiah felt when the king's messenger came to get him and in 1 Kings 22:13 said, "Behold now, the words of the prophets are unified and favorable to the king. Please let your word be like the word of one of them and speak favorably." In other words, the messenger pressured Micaiah to prophesy from his soul, rather than listen to the voice of God. He was asking him to fear man more than he feared the Lord. The way in which Micaiah chose to answer the manipulating messenger in this story constitutes a prophecy of what God is doing in the prophetic movement right now. "But Micaiah said, 'As the Lord lives, what the Lord says to me, that only will I speak.'"

A Micaiah Company is rising in the earth that will not be manipu-lated and controlled by soulish messengers and leaders who desire to flatter the people for their own sordid gain. Simply put, the Micaiah Company cannot be bought, because they have no price tag. They will prophesy the word of the Lord rather than waste time concern-ing themselves with whom it will offend or how it will personally ben-efit them.

Strange patterns
I see a trend rising in the American Church in which prophets are act-ing like, and even being treated as, magicians, prostitutes, and pimp-daddies. On stages and throughout the internet, many offer their prophetic services to anyone who can fill their pockets with money, promote their ministry and fuel book sales. These men and women are modern day prophetic whores. They find stimulation through stroking the ego and flesh of leaders and people, all at the expense of the purity and fresh anointing that we so desperately need in the prophetic movement. Like Hophni and Phinehas (I Samuel 2), these con artists are engaging in wickedness and sin in the house of God

because they treat that which is holy and pure as casual and oftentimes as a joke. The spirit of mammon has devoured these "prophets for hire". They have been ravaged by a greed for financial gain and a lust to be treated with all the perks and accommodations that a Hollywood actor would be given.

Just as Jeremiah declared in Jeremiah 23:13, many prophets in America are "prophesying by Baal" and leading the body of Christ astray. The Baal spirit has caused the prophets' focus and concern to be health, wealth, and prosperity, when they should be agonizing over the sin of the nation and travailing over how to bring forth messages of repentance, reformation, and revival. The goal has become to stroke the people to sleep, when God desires to provoke His people to change in this hour.

Financial partners

It has now become common practice in much of the prophetic movement for a prophetic voice to be directed and told to whom he or she must prophesy. Being led by the Holy Spirit and even given freedom to preach out of the Bible is becoming less accepted. Church leaders, and even prophets themselves, have begun to handpick those that they will minister to. This is not because God has a word for these people, but because they have money or position. They will be asked to sow once they "receive a word from God".

It is impossible to minister in this kind of atmosphere without partnering with the spirit of witchcraft. Many church leaders who have themselves lost the fresh anointing of the Holy Spirit and are now leading failing ministries are inviting prophets of God into their ministries in an attempt to gather large offerings and bolster their declining attendance. This sick and twisted practice not only scams the people of God, but God is nowhere to be found in the midst of this evil!

Beware of Simon the Sorcerer's

I wrote and warned in *I See A New Prophetic Generation* that a generation of Simon the Sorcerers was going to rise in the earth and radically oppose the true prophets of God. I see more of a hunger in the prophetic movement to obtain power than to walk in intimacy. I see more of a desire to live under the anointing than to demonstrate Christ-like character. I see more of an appetite to publicly prophesy over thousands than to privately pray to the Father in heaven. I see more of an obsession with chasing after someone else's prophetic mantle than with giving our time to discovering our own unique divine design given by the Father alone. I see more of an urge to chase gold dust, feathers, and angels than to encounter the Person of Jesus Christ. All of these pursuits lead to one terrifying end: The rise of a generation of "Simon the Sorcerers" who are currently operating in illegitimate authority!

These individuals carry an appearance of walking in deep relationship with Jesus, but in reality, they are collateral damage to the body of Christ. These men and women are dangerous, their motives are impure, and what they primarily pursue and emphasize causes them to live in continual dysfunction. One of the main reasons the prophetic movement is headed for shipwreck is because we are continuing to honor and give individuals positions of authority that have quit on intimacy. These prophetic individuals consistently tear down with their character what they have built with their gifting.

Supernatural Deception

I see thousands of Christian young adults in America who, like Simon the Sorcerer, are hungry for the supernatural and are therefore looking for an impartation, prayer or touch from a well-known leader in the body of Christ to launch them into their ministry. Rather than seeking intimacy with Jesus Christ and walking in true legitimate kingdom authority like Peter and John, many, just like Simon, are seeking a drive-thru experience because they are hungry for authority, but aren't willing to obtain it legally through intimacy.

Activating Charismatic Collateral Damage

Too many prophetic people are chasing after the power of God that produces the miracles and manifestations of God, but so few prophets are asking for and being taught about the trials and testing's of God that produce the character of God.

Because of this serious error in the Charismatic Movement, we have one of the most gifted, yet immoral young generations the body of Christ has ever seen. Behind this tragedy is often times too many mothers and fathers (older leaders) who are placing so much emphasis on impartation and activation in the supernatural that Christ-likeness and integrity are overlooked and not even taken seriously anymore. Have an affair on your spouse or just decide it's time to marry someone else? No problem. Children not serving the Lord yet calling for revival in America? No problem. Fornicating and drunkenness? It's all good, grace to you.

We desperately need older Christian leaders in the Charismatic Movement opening up ministry schools called, "The School of Hard Knocks", "The School of Perseverance and Character", and "The School of Suffering and Obedience". Older leaders, I implore you on behalf of my young generation to resist and rebuke this young charismatic generation of believers who want to skip the character lessons and teachings in order to "do the stuff", "get activated", and "give me your impartation" shenanigans. You are not being a spiritual father or mother to them by choosing not to address and confront character flaws. You are actually giving them permission to seriously damage themselves, their families, and the body of Christ in the days ahead.

I believe that the greatest signs, wonders, and miracles the world has ever witnessed are yet to be seen simply because God is still looking for a Micaiah Company who actually have His character to steward the power He wants to release. These will be prophetic messengers who have been severely tested, tried, and tempted and know what it means to pick up their Cross and follow Jesus. Remember, any Christian leader who does not walk with a limp because of the price that they have paid privately is not worthy to be followed publicly.

Empowering Illegitimate Authority

We who are prophets and leaders have placed so much emphasis on activation and impartation in our prophetic and supernatural schools in America, and so little time connecting people to the character and nature of God and what Jesus is really like, that we ourselves have blessed and commissioned a generation of Simon the Sorcerers who operate in illegitimate authority in the body of Christ. Because intimacy and deep union with Jesus Christ are no longer a focus in the prophetic movement, our horrendous lack of discernment has built stages for these Simon the Sorcerers and given them platforms. We have been incredibly gullible as leaders and therefore have produced extremely gullible prophetic people.

Peter told Simon the Sorcerer that his heart was not right before God. I believe Simon's desires for power and authority were not only not pleasing to God, but I believe deep within Simon's heart was an impure motive to have the apostles' hands laid on him: He was full of jealousy!

It's time to choose sides

Ahab had his 400 soulish prophets who came into agreement with false prophecy in order to please the kings, but there was one man named Micaiah who would not bow down to the man-pleasing spirit currently trying to suffocate the prophets of God. A Micaiah Company must rise in the earth who pledge allegiance to Christ and Christ alone. Their foreheads will be made of flint, like Ezekiel's. They will prophesy to the people whether they listen or fail to listen.

Throughout the Old Testament, the primary issue God had with the false prophets in Israel and Judah was that they constantly told people that they were right with God when they weren't. The false prophets would declare to those living in sin that they were at peace with God. They ignored the judgment of God and were themselves sentenced to judgment because of it.

We must begin to pray for cleansing judgment to fall upon the prophetic movement in America. Like Micaiah, perhaps the true prophets of God are actually the ones who contradict their prophetic contemporaries. The Micaiah Company will not have the largest ministries, mailing lists, or partner bases, but they will carry the word and heart of the Lord and be unashamed in declaring what the Spirit is saying. Their focus will be on prayer and intimacy with Jesus, not the supernatural and finances.

There is coming an ever widening schism within the prophetic movement and we need to thank God for it! Elijah drew the line in his day. Micaiah drew the line in his day. So it is that God is gathering a company of prophetic voices who have one thing in common. They will prophesy only what God says, nothing more and nothing less.

9
The Micaiah Company Manifesto
(Jeremiah Johnson)

GOD ALWAYS SENDS His most fiery and confrontational prophets into the darkest, driest, and most evil periods of history. Elijah, Micaiah, Jeremiah, Ezekiel, and John the Baptist are a few that come to mind whom God called to preach repentance, consecration, and reformation in a day and period of time where those types of messages were not popular or well received by the crowds. A.W. Tozer once referred to the prophets mentioned above as "religious specialists" and went on to describe their calling and the public's view of them with startling accuracy. Tozer said, "Such men were likely to be drastic, radical, possibly at times violent, and the curios crowd that gathered to watch them work soon branded them as extreme, fanatical, and negative." (*Why Revival Tarries*, Bethany House Publisher 1987 page 12)

If many in the American Church currently agree that we are living in one of the most evil periods of history, then why is there such large scale rejection, persecution, and even surprise when God Himself commissions confrontational and fiery prophets to come out of the wilderness and begin to sound the alarm in the midst of the body of Christ?

Counterbalance and reformation

I believe that we are living in a critical period of history in which we desperately need counterbalance and reformation within the prophetic movement. I receive and bless many prophets of the Lord who have been commissioned by God Himself to specifically focus on aspects of His goodness, mercy, and graciousness. We need these prophets to continue to minister the word that God has given them, but we also need to acknowledge and receive with open arms prophets who have been commissioned by God to focus specifically on aspects of His severity, justice, and righteousness. In fact, I believe that God is raising up a new breed of prophets in the earth who will have the capacity not only to minister His goodness, but also His severity. They will not pick or choose which aspects of His character and nature they prefer, but they will stand in His counsel and therefore minister His full counsel to the body of Christ.

For me personally, it has truly been a unique and eye opening experience as I continue to minister prophetically all over the United States and several foreign nations of the earth every year. I frequently discover large pockets of churches and ministries who wholeheartedly enjoy the message of the goodness of God and prophetic ministry that specifically focuses on the love and encouragement of the saints. To mention the holiness or severity of God, however, and to begin teach on the wilderness season that God calls authentic prophets into, upsets numerous people and leaders and has damaged many personal ministry relationships that I have had over the years.

Questions and answers

My heart has ached and I have lost much sleep over this one question: Why is so much of the prophetic movement and therefore the body of Christ so enthralled and obsessed with certain aspects of God's character and nature and completely opposed and turned off to other aspects of who He is? Why can I speak at prophetic conferences and minister on the love and goodness of the Father and walk out with a

$5000 love offering and then go to other prophetic conferences and minister on repentance and holiness and barely have enough money to cover my flight?

I do not claim to have all the answers, but I believe that our failures to wrestle with these difficult questions and issues within the prophetic movement have so damaged the body of Christ that I'm not sure we will ever recover. We have prophets in the prophetic movement right now who are training young prophets to believe that the discipline and chastisement of God is not New Covenant. We have forbidden and silenced the Micaiah Company in our midst who are called to bring the counterbalance and reformation that we so desperately need.

We need prophets of repentance! Where are the weepers in the prophetic movement? Where are the prophets who get invited to churches and ministries and weep over the condition of the church? Do we not realize that it will be their tears and groans that awaken the hardhearted and spiritually dead in our midst? Where are the prophets of fire? Why have we told the young prophets whom God has called to breathe fire on dry souls to tone it down so as to not offend anyone? Where are the confrontational prophets who make war on the religious spirit and call out the false prophets of Baal in the Church?

I do not know who legislated these rules, but I do know that a generation of prophets and leaders are going to have to stand before Almighty God for why they would not welcome and receive the burning, weeping, and confrontational prophetic messengers.

It would be easy at this juncture to picture these burning, weeping, and confrontational prophetic messengers as individuals who hate the body of Christ, carry severe bitterness and resentment, and are completely disconnected from church leadership, but I believe it would be a tremendous mistake to believe that. On the contrary, I believe that the reason why these prophets feel so deeply and have such unwavering conviction in their calling is that they love the body of Christ so much and desire relationship with church leadership. It is their proximity to the people of God and the shepherds of the flock that causes them to carry such a tremendous burden before God and the people.

We must identify the character traits and the nature of the call upon the lives of the Micaiah Company so that we can not only welcome them with eager expectation, but also embrace the mandate that they carry for the body of Christ in this hour. The following seven earmarks of the Micaiah Company are my small attempt through prayer and fasting to paint a profile for these prophets, not to box them in, but to help release clarity and exposure to the calling that is upon their lives. I believe that the need for these prophets within the prophetic movement and the release upon the body of Christ has never been greater.

1. Fiery and Confrontational

The Micaiah Company is comprised of individuals who preach and prophesy repentance and reform. These burning ones carry a message of spiritual awakening that confronts darkness and releases refreshing wherever they go. The Jewish scholar, Abraham Heschel, rightly describes the nature of these types of prophets when he writes and says, "The prophet is human, yet he employs notes one octave too high for our ears. He experiences moments that defy our understanding. He is neither 'a singing saint' nor 'a moralizing poet', but an assaulter of the mind. Often his words begin to burn where conscience ends." (*The Prophets,* Harper/Perenial Modern Classics Publisher, 1962 page 12)

When a voice from within the Micaiah Company speaks, it will be distinct and will often carry a sobering message of truth that cuts to the hearts of men and gives them a divine opportunity to get right with God.

The mouths of the Micaiah Company are sharp swords. Their prophetic words are polished arrows taken from the quiver of God (Isaiah 49:2). These messengers are specifically equipped and more than ready to confront the false prophets of Baal. They have a distaste for those who intentionally lead the body of Christ astray with words of false hope and flattery when God has called for repentance. The Micaiah Company have fire in their bones and they will not rest day or night until they witness and testify to the plans and purposes of God established in the earth. They indeed will know their God as the One who answers by fire!

2. Wilderness Trained

The Micaiah Company has been forged in the wilderness where they have accepted the invitation from Above to pick up their cross and follow Jesus. These men and women fully understand the years of trial, testing, and temptation that are required to bear the markings of a Micaiah. Because of their perseverance in the secret place, God has given them great authority when they open up their mouths in the public place. It is in the wilderness where authentic prophets find their voice. They learn how to die to their selfish ambition, pride, arrogance and carnal dreams and become dependent upon God for everything.

It is quite easy to spot a member of the Micaiah company because they walk with a limp and carry a message of brokenness and humility. The excruciating suffering that they have been through is not due to the sin in their lives, but is a result of the intense call upon their lives. They have been rejected, despised, persecuted by their brethren, and often exposed to great family turmoil.

The way in which God has provided for many in the Micaiah Company is supernatural. Even as God used ravens, a widow and angels to provide for Elijah the prophet, many of those trained in the wilderness have had to be humbled and broken time and time again so they might learn what it means to live on every word that comes from the mouth of God.

The Micaiah Company is not only familiar with the wilderness, but they invite others to partake of it. These are the prophets who bid the masses to come and die to themselves so that the Spirit of God might live through them. The centrality of the Cross and its glory in the wilderness season is a primary message trumpeted by the Micaiah Company.

3. Messengers of Justice, Righteousness, and Holiness

The Micaiah Company understands, easily embraces, and declares aspects of God's character and nature that are very difficult for the masses to absorb. Simply the way in which these messengers have chosen to conduct themselves sends a warning message to any that would cross their path. These are men and women who live a radical lifestyle of holiness and consecration to the Lord. They are lovesick for the Bridegroom and have been ravished by His heart.

When they prophesy, they expose and tear down idols and vain imaginations raised up against the greatness of God. True prophetic preaching confronts worldly ideologies concerning the justice, righteousness, and holiness of God.

The Micaiah Company spends their time joining the four living creatures in the throne room as they cry out, "Holy!" for all of eternity. Because of their fierce dedication and conviction to live a life separated from the world, the Micaiah Company is constantly accused of being legalistic, judgmental, negative, critical and insensitive. They are a group misunderstood by many and their passion to see a pure and spotless Bride presented to the Bridegroom at the end of the Age drives religious hypocrites crazy.

The Micaiah Company is despised by the health, wealth, and prosperity camp in America. Those who want a quick experience of crucifixion so they can enjoy a long life of resurrection hate the Micaiah Company. They cannot stand their words that continually call the crowds to greater depths of holiness and righteousness.

The justice of God and His unwillingness to turn the other way while nations, individuals, and the body of Christ live a lifestyle of sin is a premier message that the Micaiah Company declares and false prophets cannot stand. False prophets speak when God has not spoken and run when He has not sent them. False prophets tell nations, individuals, and the body of Christ that God is at peace with them when in fact He is not. False prophets declare that God is in a good mood all the time when millions of babies are being aborted, gay marriage is legalized, and a slew of other issues are at hand.

In essence, while false prophets make everyone feel at ease in hours of crisis, the Micaiah Company sounds the alarm and begins to focus on intensifying the responsibility for sin in the body of Christ. These prophetic messengers carry shock and awe capability. When they open up their mouths to declare the justice of God, the fear of the Lord overtakes entire gatherings of people. It's as if they possess clarity regarding the mind and heart of God toward key issues in society, while everyone else remains blind to the sin in the land.

The Micaiah Company will confront people, leaders, and nations with the Holy One of Israel! Their primary message will be centered upon repentance and reform. What others are calling "revival", these prophetic messengers will weep over. They are not pursuing miracles and people getting slain in the spirit. The Micaiah Company will inquire, "Where is the standard of righteousness and trumpet call to holy living?" They will ask, "Where are the altars full of people groaning and travailing over their sins and the sin of this nation?"

In the words of the prophet Isaiah found in chapter thirty verses nine through eleven and verse fifteen,

> "These are rebellious people, deceitful children, children unwilling to listen to the Lord's instruction. They say to the seers, "See no more visions!" and to the prophets, "Give us no more visions of what is right! Tell us pleasant things, prophesy illusions. Leave this way, get off this path, and STOP CONFRONTING US WITH THE HOLY ONE OF ISRAEL!" This is what the Sovereign Lord, the Holy One of Israel says: "In REPENTANCE and rest is your salvation, in quietness and trust is your strength, but you would have none of it."

The Micaiah Company will not settle for worldly sorrow, but hunger for godly repentance!

4. Jesus-centered

We are currently witnessing one of the greatest debacles in the history of the prophetic movement and it's this: the exaltation, focus, and empowerment of demons and principalities and spiritual bankruptcy among a generation of prophets concerning the glorious person of Jesus Christ. There is so much insight being offered concerning evil spirits, but yet so little revelation in regard to the kingdom of God and His Son, the Lord Jesus Christ.

According to Revelation 19:10, it is the TESTIMONY OF JESUS that is the spirit of prophecy, not the testimony of Jezebel, Judas, Saul, Absalom or any other "spirit". We are observing a growing number of "prophets" who incessantly give themselves to exposing and declaring the spirit of this and the spirit of that to the body of Christ. Meanwhile there is no trumpeting of the person of Jesus Christ! Not only that, but there are hardly any messages being released on His life, death, burial, resurrection, ascension, or His second coming. Many contemporary prophets are now becoming "spiritual warfare centered" rather than "Jesus centered". Because of this epidemic, knowingly or unknowingly, these individuals are releasing paranoia, distraction, and misfocus to the body of Christ by consistently choosing to highlight, and therefore empower evil, rather than releasing wisdom and revelation concerning the beautiful One, Jesus!

Out of all the apostolic prayers that Paul prayed in the New Testament, ZERO address any demonic spirit, word curse, mind curse, body curse, generational curse, soul curse, spirit curse, curse, curse, curse (you get the point). We must return to biblical foundations in the prophetic movement and stop all the nonsense. We must have prophets rise in the earth who will accept the invitation to position themselves before the throne mentioned in Revelation 4 and behold the beauty and magnificence of Jesus.

If the four living creatures were to appear at our next prophetic gathering in America, I'm certain they would trumpet what they continually behold and place infinite value in: the One who sits on the throne! It's time for a holy pause and a reset in the contemporary prophetic movement. We must shift our attention away from the spirit of this and the spirit of that, stop calling it prophecy and start gazing upon the Son of Man to make His name great in the earth! The Micaiah Company will spend their days gazing upon the beauty of Jesus and declaring His infinite worth to all those who will listen. He is their preoccupation, obsession, reward, and one heart's desire.

5. No Fear of Man
The Micaiah Company has Daniel's Den loyalty to the word of the Lord and will not bend to the political spirit that is sweeping the prophetic movement and much of the body of Christ. Just as Micaiah stood as one prophet against 400 prophets in his day, so I believe the odds are much steeper in twenty first century. Much of what the Micaiah Company will trumpet as the word of the Lord will contradict their prophetic contemporaries and bring scorn from those who want to be tickled with the latest and greatest revelation that puts them to sleep by pacifying any desire they might have to get right with God.

The Micaiah Company cannot be bought. There is no amount of money nor offer that they will take to compromise the word of the Lord. They fear the Lord more than they fear man. They crave the acceptance and applause of the Father more than they worry about the rejection of men. Micaiah Company prophets do not tell the body of Christ what they want to hear. Rather, they declare what they need to hear. In other terms, the Micaiah Company hands out vegetables that help individuals grow healthy and mature while the masses cry out for false prophets to give them sugar-coated words that cater to the fleshly desires of men and produce little to no fruit.

6. Travail and Intercession
The Micaiah Company has been forged in the context of night and day prayer. These individuals prefer the prayer room more than they do the platform. They actually get disappointed when they have to minister publicly because they enjoy the counsel of the Lord that much privately. The Micaiah Company are groaners and weepers. These men

and women travail in the place of prayer and fasting and give birth in the spirit before they ever manifest in the natural. Many of the public meetings and conferences that the Micaiah Company prophets are asked to lead somehow always turn into prayer meetings.

The Micaiah Company are not obsessed or impressed with their prophetic gifting, but rather place it on the altar of the Lord. In fact, they are so committed to operating in the fresh anointing of the Holy Spirit that they refuse to prophesy to anyone unless they have spent considerable time in prayer. They choose to steward and govern their prophetic gifts from the safety of travail and intercession. These prophetic messengers live down on their knees and just don't carry the word of the Lord, but possess the burden of the word of the Lord.

One of the greatest assets the Micaiah Company can offer the body of Christ is this: tears! They will weep and wail over the sinful condition of the church and anguish over the blindness and hard-heartedness of this generation. While others are laughing, these prophets will be crying. These men and women feel fiercely and have learned how to fellowship with the emotions of God to discover how He is about to act in a moment of time. One of the primary callings of the Micaiah company is to conquer the callousness of the body of Christ through the ministry of weeping and travail.

7. Friends of the Bride

Although the Micaiah Company derives its name from an Old Testament prophet, the prophetic ministry has radically shifted and been upgraded at the establishing of the New Covenant by the shed blood of Jesus Christ on Calvary. Perhaps the primary difference in Old Covenant and New Covenant prophecy is regarding how prophets are now called to relate to others.

In the Old Covenant, the prophets were the singular voice of God to the nation. They held an office and position of authority in the Old Covenant that they do not currently hold under the New Covenant. Old Covenant prophets were given permission to be disconnected from the people and often appeared on the scene with little to no relationship with anyone. Under the New Covenant, prophets are now established members of the body of Christ and can no longer operate out of an Old Covenant mindset that allows them to be lone rangers and, in many cases, do collateral damage to many portions of the Church.

The Micaiah Company is not a group of individuals who do not attend church. They don't carry serious wounds toward church leadership. This is not a company of rejects who can't stand order and authority. The Micaiah Company in no way, shape, or fashion gives prophets permission to be rebellious, harsh, mean, and unaccountable to the body of Christ and church leaders. The truth is that the Micaiah Company are men and women who are friends of the Bride of Christ and deeply love her! Yes, there will be confrontation with those who are treating the bride of Christ wrongly, those who are abusing her, and using her for sordid gain, but the Micaiah Company are prophets who have joined themselves to the body of Christ and consider themselves as part of her.

Many of these prophets are not necessarily well liked by the masses, but they do have widespread influence among a remnant of people and leaders who are hungry to receive the word of the Lord regardless of what it is. These remnant communities of believers and leaders will provide great safety and encouragement to the Micaiah Company.

Pray for the prophetic movement
Being recognized as part of the Micaiah Company is not a matter of spiritual pride or prophetic elitism. It is not a license to boast or permission to act foolishly. It is simply a term that is being used to help identify those in the prophetic movement that God is raising up for such a time as this. We must constantly keep our eyes peeled and ears open for timely truth that will assist us in staying clear of deception and remaining current with what God is saying and doing in this hour. May we continue to pray for the prophetic movement and its prophets. Let us seek repentance and reconciliation from God

Himself for why we have so openly endorsed and embraced certain portions of prophetic ministry and completely ignored and discarded others. I see counterbalance and reformation returning to the prophetic movement, and the body of Christ continuing to be healed and restored because of it.

10
Parting Shot: A Prophetic Word of Application

(R. Loren Sandford)

IN RECENT DAYS, evangelical and charismatic Christians have raised an ever more desperate cry to God to save America, to restore the nation to Him and pull us out of the pit into which we have fallen before it's too late. By extension, this aptly applies to the rest of the world influenced by the culture we share. Toward this end, great gatherings of prayer have sprung up in various places. I thank God for this, but prayer alone cannot win the day, and effective prayer needs an effective focus.

The key to the salvation of this nation and the world lies squarely in the hands of the church. Despite the protestations of those who have abandoned the organized church, we cannot revive the nation without first reviving the church. Herein lies a primary calling for the Micaiah Company. Only the bride without spot or wrinkle (Ephesians 5:27) can prevail in this day and we must speak into her cleansing. With very few exceptions (and I acknowledge a few), every revival that has ever swept this nation has begun in the church and been sustained by and through the church. Historically, revival begins in the church and then works its way into the surrounding culture.

For example, the First Great Awakening under Jonathan Edwards in the early 18th century began in his church in Northampton, Massachusetts and then spread to the other colonies, eventually changing the surrounding culture and influencing the values on which the nation was founded. We would include him in the Micaiah Company if he were alive today. He brought revival by confronting sin in the strongest terms.

The Second Great Awakening in the early 19th century likewise began in the church in Baptist and Methodist congregations. Again, the surrounding culture experienced radical transformation. When the Holy Spirit fell in the Cane Ridge camp meetings during that period of time, repentance from sin was a major focus. Apparently, there have been Micaiahs blazing a trail before us. The Azusa Street revival beginning in 1906 that birthed Pentecostalism likewise broke out in the church and was sustained in the church. This is the history of revival in America.

I don't believe we will see a revived America - and the cultures and nations affected by America - before we see truly revived churches. As goes the church, so goes the nation. Overall, however, the church in this nation has increasingly fallen into sickness while huge numbers of people vote with their feet, many of them filled with emotions ranging from disappointment to bitterness. How desperately we need a Micaiah Company to speak words of life with the power to deliver the Ahabs of our day from unnecessary death.

The sickness afflicting the church is both moral and doctrinal. In too many places - including many influential mega-churches - basic morality, godliness and holiness, clearly stated in Scripture and historically accepted, have not been taught or understood as extensions and expressions of the Father's love. Rather, they have often been rejected as mere religious-spirited rules and sources of condemnation to be discarded or reinterpreted in accord with the world's concept of mercy or political correctness.

In lockstep with this erosion of core values, an increasing state of fatherlessness has fed a culture that understands neither the true heart of God nor the meaning of covenant. Lawlessness and love-lessness then result as families disintegrate and God's beloveds find themselves deprived of a sense of heritage, calling and transcendent purpose. Scripturally, these things are fruits of a father's blessing. The Micaiah Company cannot be born and thrive without a remnant of Elijahs, an older generation of seasoned, humbled and fearless voices who understand what it is to father the fatherless with the heart of the Father. Let these arise!

Doctrinally, a Great Apostasy has been gathering steam as the foundation of the Word of God has been compromised or denied in ministry after ministry and in many influential mega-churches. Core doctrines such as the sovereignty of God, the existence of hell, the substitutionary sacrifice of Jesus and other core elements of our faith are being rejected or reinterpreted. Once more, this is the way of a fatherless culture that fails to pass heritage and blessing from generation to generation. We then wonder why society seems to be collapsing, crime rates rise and our children are lost to us. The founda-tions have been destroyed. God is sending Micaiahs in the spirit and power of Elijah (mixed metaphor...) to strengthen the weak, repair the damage being done and "restore all things" (Matthew 17:11).

We don't need more manifestations and esoteric spiritual teach-ings in the church designed to give us an experience we call revival. Although I love supernatural manifestations and stand steadfastly against the critics who deny them, what we need is a church infused with the selfless and loving heart of Father God. We need a church that understands the love behind every law and principle embedded in every line of Scripture handed down by God to enable us to live well. We need a church that reveals to the world how to apply these things relationally in love without altering the meaning or ignoring the content.

The revival to come therefore takes us beyond the teaching of the Father's love for remedial inner healing that has been the dominant approach to this subject in recent decades. We needed that message and still do, but it doesn't take us far enough. The revival to come will bring a new level of revelation of the Father's love that releases life, carries God's people beyond themselves in selfless sacrifice, imparts real purpose and enables them to rise higher into their destinies and callings. It's not so much about healing as it is about what we're becoming in Him as we conform to the image of the Son (Romans 8:29). We Micaiahs don't just cry against sin. We cry *for* transformation and the glory that comes with it.

In the Father's heart we each inherit a high calling and purpose from the Savior who longs for His children to do greater things than He did. "Truly, truly, I say to you, he who believes in Me, the works that I do, he will do also; and greater works than these he will do; because I go to the Father" (John 14:12). Every true father wants his children to rise above his own level of achievement or happiness in life and empowers and releases them to do so. Let prophets and leaders arise in the body of Christ who carry that heart, impart real life and truly set God's people free.

While I see a growing number of pastors and leaders whose character radiates the heart of the Father in relation to the people they lead, I also hear increasing stories of abuse, lack of love, domination and control. Fatherless leaders lead fatherlessly. Fatherless prophets prophesy cheaply and inaccurately. As a result, without a vision, the people perish. We have suffered a generation of concerted attack on the institution of fatherhood and now we pay the price in leaders of government, schools, businesses and the church who cannot father. Prophets who cannot father cannot truly love. They end up as noisy gongs and clanging cymbals, as Paul so aptly stated in I Corinthians 13:1). Because they cannot father, life is cut off, chaos grows and society suffers. If ever there was a time for Malachi 4:5-6 to be fulfilled, it is now. "Behold, I am going to send you Elijah the prophet before the coming of the great and terrible day of the Lord. He will restore the hearts of the fathers to their children and the hearts of the children to their fathers, so that I will not come and smite the land with a curse."

Let revival begin in the church, but let it be a revival energized and centered in a revelation of the heart of Father God the like of which we have never seen. This the call of the Micaiah Company. Let this revelation revolutionize the character of leadership and the body of Christ in a way that transforms the way the world sees the church. Let it revolutionize leadership styles. Let a life-giving spirit flow from the hearts of a rising generation of prophets and leaders who, by their character imparted from the heart and spirit of a loving God, release freedom, life, heritage and destiny into the people of God. Then watch those people change their nation and their world.

About the Authors

Jeremiah Johnson is a graduate of Southeastern University in Lakeland, FL where he earned his bachelors degree in Church Ministries. He planted Heart of the Father Ministry in Lakeland, FL and is on the Eldership team. A gifted teacher, book author, and prophetic minister, Jeremiah travels nationally and internationally as a conference and guest speaker. Check out his most recent book, *I See: A New Prophetic Generation*, on his website www.beholdthemanministries.com. Jeremiah and his wife, Morgan, reside in Florida with their three children

R. Loren Sandford graduated from Fuller Theological Seminary with a Masters of Divinity Degree. He is senior pastor of New Song Church and Ministries in Denver, CO. He speaks nationally and internationally and has written several books, including, *Purifying the Prophetic, Understanding Prophetic People, The Prophetic Church*, and *Yes, There is More*. He and his wife, Beth, live in Colorado.

To find out more information concerning where Jeremiah and Loren are ministering next, please visit www.themicaiahcompany.com. You can also follow them by liking and following the Micaiah Company Facebook page.